I0891921

P.S. I Love You

P.S. I Love You

The Story of the Singing Hilltoppers

Carlton Jackson

THE UNIVERSITY PRESS OF KENTUCKY

Publication of this volume was made possible in part by a grant from the National Endowment for the Humanities.

Copyright © 2007 by The University Press of Kentucky

Scholarly publisher for the Commonwealth, serving Bellarmine University, Berea College, Centre College of Kentucky, Eastern Kentucky University, The Filson Historical Society, Georgetown College, Kentucky Historical Society, Kentucky State University, Morehead State University, Murray State University, Northern Kentucky University, Transylvania University, University of Kentucky, University of Louisville, and Western Kentucky University.
All rights reserved.

Editorial and Sales Offices: The University Press of Kentucky
663 South Limestone Street, Lexington, Kentucky 40508-4008
www.kentuckypress.com

11 10 09 08 07 5 4 3 2 1

Library of Congress Cataloging-in-Publication Data

Jackson, Carlton.
P.S. I love you : the story of the singing Hilltoppers / Carlton Jackson.
p. cm.
Includes bibliographical references, discography, and index.
ISBN-13: 978-0-8131-2436-0 (hardcover : alk. paper)
ISBN-10: 0-8131-2436-0 (hardcover : alk. paper) 1. Hilltoppers (Musical group) 2. Singers—United States—Biography. I. Title.
ML421.H54J33 2007
782.42164092'2—dc22
[B] 2006039705

This book is printed on acid-free recycled paper meeting the requirements of the American National Standard for Permanence in Paper for Printed Library Materials.

Manufactured in the United States of America.

Member of the Association of
American University Presses

To Hilltoppers,
whoever and wherever you may be.

Contents

The Hilltoppers

Two Appreciations

I was pleased to be asked by Carlton Jackson to write an introduction about Billy Vaughn and the Hilltoppers. I knew each of them personally, and we were classmates at Western Kentucky University together. I had known Billy Vaughn and played with his group before I met the other guys. Billy was an older musician who played with Ace Dinning's band at the Boots and Saddle nightclub on the edge of Bowling Green. Billy's daytime job was cutting hair to support his family. Billy's big talent was arranging and composing.

At Western in my sophomore year (1948), I reorganized the Red and Grey dance band and this group played for many parties, dances, and other functions on and off campus. In my last year at Western (1951), Jimmy Sacca came in as a freshman music major on a football scholarship. I hired him to sing in the Red and Grey Band, but I had to replace him because he would not learn any new songs. Seymour Spiegelman was also a music major. Don McGuire played on Western's basketball team.

After I graduated in 1951, I moved to the University of Kentucky, Frankfort, the state's capital, and Ohio State University and then back to Western to be on its music faculty. My relationship resumed with Billy Vaughn as before, doing many gigs, including tours to Japan with his Hollywood band in 1986 and 1987.

The Hilltoppers recorded their first song with a portable tape recorder in Van Meter Auditorium. The song was "Trying," a ballad that made them famous. It was just my luck to have missed out on their early years, but I kept up with the group and was very proud of their making the hit parade numerous times. Their beautiful and original songs and arrangements made them a national hit. I still have a dance orchestra and I still get requests for Hilltoppers' songs.

The author, Carlton Jackson, wanted me to try to compare the contemporary popular music of today to yesterday's Hilltoppers. To me, there is no comparison. I've found that the older generations (myself included) still like the tunes that the Hilltoppers sang back then.

Doc Livingston

Jimmy Sacca, Lockport, New York; Don McGuire, Hazard, Kentucky; Billy Vaughn, Glasgow, Kentucky; and Seymour Spiegelman, Seneca Falls, New York. How did four guys with such diverse backgrounds get together to begin singing? The common ground, of course, was Western Kentucky University, where they were students.

It was easy for the four to get acquainted on Western's campus. In 1952, there were about fifteen hundred students, and since two of the four were scholarship athletes (Jimmy Sacca, football, end; and Don McGuire, basketball, guard), everybody knew them from the beginning. Because of Western's rich tradition in athletics, especially basketball, students, faculty, and staff alike attended all the games.

Western had some great moments and outstanding accomplishments through its evolution from 1906, when it was founded as Western Kentucky State Normal School, to 1966, when it became Western Kentucky University, and beyond. Let me mention a few that are my favorites: number one in the world in debate; number one in the world in journalism; more than $100 million contributed in the very first capital campaign, Investing in the Spirit; national champion female gymnast; an astronaut (Terry Wilcutt) with a red towel (recalling basketball coach Ed Diddle's waving a red towel during games) in the cockpit on his trips into space; national champion football team in 2002; NCAA Final Four in men's basketball in 1971; and the NCAA championship game in women's basketball in 1992. (This is a random listing and certainly not necessarily in order of importance.)

None of these ranks any higher than the Hilltoppers' appearance that Sunday evening in 1952 in New York City on Toast of the Town, hosted by Ed Sullivan. It was with great anticipation that the student body and Westerners everywhere waited for the four guys with their striped beanies crowning youthful faces to appear onstage.

Television was in its infancy, and black and white ruled the screen. Very few homes were blessed with television sets, and sets were really scarce around campus, so groups assembled to watch the Sullivan broadcast. Simultaneous roars echoed across "the Hill" as our heroes appeared from behind the stage curtains. It was a sound not unlike the roar of the crowd that I heard at my one and only bullfight when the matador entered the ring or when Western hit a basket at the horn to win by one.

This feeling of pride lasted for the next few years as the Hilltoppers soared on the music charts, including the million-sellers chart, and as they entertained live from London to Tokyo with stops in New York, Las Vegas, and other cities throughout the United States.

The author, my friend Carlton Jackson, one of the most published faculty members at Western and in the southeastern United States, has books on a wide range of subjects. He has not limited his writings to his specialized discipline, history, but has covered the waterfront. The only common thread is that all his books are so readable. This book about the Hilltoppers is no exception.

Lee Robertson

Introduction

My interest in the singing Hilltoppers goes back at least to 1986. I was at a social function one night, and Doc Livingston was in attendance. The conversation got off onto the Hilltoppers, and a guest remarked, "Somebody ought to write a book about them." Doc pointed his finger straight at me and said, "Carlton, you write books. Why don't you do it?" I replied, "Set me up with them, and we'll see what happens."

This was the prelude to a long lunch with Billy Vaughn at Bowling Green, Kentucky's, Parakeet Restaurant that went deep into the afternoon. He told me about his musical career, and I expressed the desire to write about him and Jimmy Sacca, Seymour Spiegelman, and Don McGuire, the original Hilltoppers. After I agreed to look further into the subject, other things intervened. I was working on a couple of other projects at the time, and the Hilltoppers would have to wait. Then, not all that long after the lunch, I learned that Billy had moved back to California. The singing Hilltoppers, though, always stayed in the back of my mind as a most worthy subject to write about.

Then in 2003 I learned that Bobbie Ann Mason, the Hilltoppers' first national fan-club president, had loaned her Hilltopper materials to the archives at Western Kentucky University. And there was this wonderful exhibit at the Kentucky Museum about the Hilltoppers organized and arranged by Sue Lynn McDaniel of the University Archives. Also, a new Hilltoppers CD was released, and Jimmy Sacca came to campus. All this activity put me into a frame of mind to pick up where I had left off back in 1986. This book is the result.

By early 2004, both Jimmy Sacca and Don McGuire lived in Lexington, Kentucky, and were most cooperative in granting interviews, answering my numerous letters and e-mails, and allowing me to visit them in their homes. I have now had the privilege of meeting three of the original four Hilltoppers (Billy Vaughn, Jimmy Sacca, and Don McGuire). Seymour Spiegelman is the only one I never met personally, but through his daughters, Penny and Sueellyn, and his brother, Irwin, I have come to know quite a bit about him.

I asked two old friends and colleagues at WKU, Doc Livingston and Lee Robertson, to write forewords for the book. Doc and Lee knew the original Hilltoppers. Doc knew them primarily from a musical viewpoint, playing with them in various bands. Lee probably knows more about the internal workings of Western than anyone else on campus. He joined Kelly Thompson early on in befriending and publicizing the singing Hilltoppers. I believe Doc and Lee help considerably in putting my book into a campus perspective. I thank both of them for honoring me with their forewords.

While I was working on this manuscript, I told a friend that I had written enough sad books in my career. I wanted this one to be a happy book. I sincerely believe it is. I hope to reach several levels of reading audiences. Of course, local readers, especially those with connections to Western Kentucky University and Bowling Green, should have an interest here. I believe this book will also resonate with readers in south-central Kentucky and throughout the commonwealth.

I do not, however, intend this book to be labeled only as local, or even as regional. It has a universal subject. One must remember that the singing Hilltoppers enjoyed worldwide fame. Many fans still actively pursue their music in England, Germany, France, South Africa, Australia, and Japan, to say nothing of the United States. Also, the fact that one of the original Hilltoppers, Billy Vaughn, went on to great prominence as a bandleader and music arranger helped to keep the group in the spotlight.

How do the Hilltoppers speak to us today? As I try to explain in subsequent pages, singing groups like the Hilltoppers always benefit from the waves of nostalgia that wash over the country from to time. In the eighties, many Americans pined for the fifties; in the nineties, the seventies were looked back upon with fondness, and so far in the first decade of the twenty-first century, the eighties in retrospect look like good years. Music is always a part of nostalgia, and this is where the Hilltoppers come in. Who knows what the next episode of nostalgia will be? If it is for the late fifties and early sixties, the Hilltoppers have got it made.

No matter how prominent a group is, it still has to have its product publicized; people have to know that it's out there. Pretty, tuneful, harmonizing, storytelling songs are works of art. When you are exposed to them, you generally take to them well. Again, this is where the singing Hilltoppers come into focus. Superstar Stevie Wonder rightly says, "Music is a world within itself, with a language which all understand." As sociologist Simon Frith explains, "Regardless of the social class of the listener . . . music functions . . . as a way of defining the self . . . bringing about collective excitement, sense of solidarity, and subcultural consciousness." It is the "longing for emotions," as another sociologist, Theodor Adorno, tells us, that keeps people around the world listening to "popular music," which is *so* popular, Adorno says, that "it holds the patent on the spirit of the times." With their love songs and tuneful ballads, the singing Hilltoppers helped an immediate post–World War II generation deal with phenomena such as "Crockettmania" (brought on by TV shows about Davy Crockett, hero of the Alamo), identical houses (the best movie on this is Martin Ritt's *No Down Payment*), the Mickey Mouse Club, the Edsel, Nikita Khrushchev, Camelot, Marilyn Monroe, John Glenn, the *Brown* decision, the twist, rock 'n' roll, and various international crises, which seem always to be with us.[1]

Throughout the history of this country, it has been asserted that the United States is the land of opportunity. "Regardless of the conditions of birth or national origin, one can be whatever one wishes to be," or go as far as one's talents will permit. One wonders where the original Hilltoppers would have gone if the U.S. military draft and other occurrences explained in the text had not intervened. The fact that these four young men could rise so high in so short a time from 1952 to the early 1960s is testament to the truth of famous French writer Alexis de Tocqueville's observation that class distinctions did not develop in the New World, as they had always existed in the old. There were new opportunities, new avenues of achievement, and the singing Hilltoppers definitely took advantage of them.[2]

The singing Hilltoppers made the word "Hilltopper" (Western's nickname) applicable year-round. They were not limited to athletic seasons. They brought fame and honor to themselves and to their alma mater, Bowling Green, the state of Kentucky, the country, and the world. It has been a pleasure to research and write this book about the singing Hilltoppers.

Chapter 1, "'Trying' Times," starts with the singing Hilltoppers on the stage of the Ed Sullivan show, in some ways the first public appearance the four had made together. Then we shift to Western Kentucky State Teachers' College and one of its recent graduates, Billy Vaughn. He had written a song called "Trying" and enlisted the help of his friend, football player Jimmy Sacca, to record it. They did, in Van Meter Auditorium on the Western campus, and the song garnered great fame for these four young men—two from New York and two from Kentucky—in the years ahead. In fact, it became their signature song.

The trials and tribulations of being a singing Hilltopper are described in "A Gathering of Hilltoppers," chapter 2. How did North and South meet as one in the singing Hilltoppers? How did these young men keep up their classroom responsibilities while at the same time performing, mostly on weekends, all over the country? It was an impressive balancing act.

Chapter 3, "'Mixed-up' Hilltoppers," deals primarily with the Korean War, when the original Hilltoppers were broken apart, a fact that was to have significant consequences for the singing group in the years ahead. Jimmy Sacca was the first to be drafted into the army, followed by Seymour Spiegelman and Don McGuire. These conscriptions led to the addition of singers to the Hilltoppers. These additions were talented young people, but they could not really fill the shoes of the original singers. Fan clubs kept waiting for the reunion of Vaughn, Sacca, Spiegelman, and McGuire. It did happen, at least in a way, but was not all that pleasing to Hilltopper fans.

Chapter 4 deals primarily with the Hilltoppers' first singing tour to England in 1956 and all of the cultural shocks they encountered, including driving on the left side of the road and the "peculiar" accent of the English. Despite a few negative reviews, the singing Hilltoppers were tremendously popular throughout the British Isles.

Chapter 5 discusses "the charts," how Hilltopper songs fared throughout the country, and how these songs compared with those by other jukebox and recording artists. This chapter also shows how charts, primarily those from *Billboard,* are made and why people interested in American popular music should pay some attention to them. Included here, too, is a discussion of "cover" or "white cover" records, which were part of the recording industry for a few years in the late fifties and early sixties, a system in recording manipulated by Randy Wood of Dot Records. Also in this chapter is a discussion of how the Hilltoppers sang the theme song from a popular movie of the day, *The Kentuckian,* adding to their national and international reputations.

By 1957, Hilltopper fortunes were declining; this is the theme of chapter 6, "The Hilltoppers at Home and Abroad." The original Hilltoppers did come back together, which thrilled fan clubs and audiences throughout the country, especially in the East, where they were primarily known. But time had passed them by, and it wasn't their fault. The military draft took away three of them during their heyday, and this had serious repercussions for their lives and careers. Other factors certainly could and should be included in an examination of the Hilltoppers' demise, and they are fully discussed in the pages ahead.

Chapter 7, "Latter-Day Hilltoppers," explains the further decline not only of the original group but also of all those who sang as Hilltoppers. Jimmy Sacca tried to keep the group alive, but his efforts were not, over the long haul, successful. The group still had some glory moments, though, as when, in 1972, they returned to the Hill for the Forty-third Homecoming, to the thorough delight of the home crowd and citizens from all over the commonwealth. Later, all four original members of the Hilltoppers were inducted into the WKU Hall of Fame, two of them (Billy Vaughn and Seymour Spiegelman) posthumously. This chapter also offers an analysis of the singing Hilltoppers and their significance to the early years of the twenty-first century.

Throughout this book, I have tried to strike a balance between narrative and analysis. I hope I have succeeded. I believe I have succeeded.

1 "Trying" Times

Toast of the Town for October 26, 1952, was, as host Ed Sullivan always said, "a really big shew." Headlining the event was veteran comedian and actor Joe E. Brown, who kept the audience chuckling by performing some vaudeville routines and playing doctor and nurse. Also on board were famed violinist Yehudi Menuhin, popular singer Connie Russell, and actor Henry Fonda. A group of young ladies from the Midwest played xylophones. Altogether it was just one more Sunday evening of great entertainment from the CBS television network.

About the middle of the program Sullivan introduced a new group of singers, calling them a "glamorous story of the song-writing business." They bounced out on the stage wearing beanies, white buckskin shoes, and gray flannel pants. Each wore a somewhat oversized maroon sweater, upon which was emblazoned a large W.[1]

Billy Vaughn was the oldest of the four. He wore his beanie almost over his forehead, to keep a receding hairline from attracting too much attention. During the performance, Billy, the most experienced of the players, kept moving his fingers as though he were keeping time to the beat instead of showing how nervous he was. He later admitted that "he felt rather silly up there [on the stage] . . . dressed in a little red and white beanie and a red sweater with a big white W on it."[2]

Next to Billy was Don McGuire, who kept looking up at the ceiling and out into the balcony audience. His beanie, unlike Billy's, was on the back of his head, not obscuring but enhancing his blond hair, pug nose, and general good looks. He had few smiles to offer here. Nonetheless, before the show, just as though he were a seasoned veteran, he wired his brother, Bobby: "Hitting New York Tonight: Ed Sullivan Show."[3]

Jimmy Sacca, the lead singer, came next in the formation. As he had done before and would again in the future, Jimmy closed his eyes as he went through the rhythms of "Trying," a ballad written by Vaughn. As Jimmy sang, the others swayed and hummed behind him. As one writer reported, with some understatement, "Jimmy's experience was evident"—he had performed previously in Bowling Green and other places—but the rest of the "swaying" Hilltoppers appeared "a bit star-struck."[4]

The last of the foursome was Seymour "Sy" Spiegelman, who actually looked ill, as though he were stifling a belch. He and Jimmy kept weaving in and out of their spaces, and both Sy and Don gave every appearance during this performance that they would be glad when it was over. Sy kept looking out into an area offstage where some mysterious shadows moved back and forth. A lone piano accompanied the four as they finally could sing the end, "but you can't blame a fellow for trying," and make their way offstage. Ed Sullivan autographed Billy Vaughn's copy of "Trying," writing: "Hi—You don't have to try any more—you're home." They got a handsome round of applause from the New York crowd, and Sullivan said to all four of them, "Great job, guys!" The "guys" were the Hilltoppers from Western Kentucky State College in Bowling Green, and they would go on to much fame in the years ahead.[5]

One reason for their nervousness on the Ed Sullivan show—maybe the only one—was that they had never performed before a large audience. They were used to singing to coeds on campus, at local supper clubs, and at sponsored events. Now here they were before a studio audience of maybe a thousand people and a television audience of some 40 million viewers. That was, as one person put it, a "hell of a way" to break into the public consciousness.

They traveled to New York by auto. Driving the Buick that Jimmy's parents had let him bring to campus, the group left Bowling Green on Thursday, October 23, and arrived in Manhattan two days later. They returned to Bowling Green in the early morning hours of Tuesday, October 28. Billy was not keen on flying; for all the concerts that lay in the future, Billy would leave three or four days early to go by rail. The other three usually went by a plane piloted by Wilbur Parrish, who owned a charter flight service in Louisville.[6]

They knew before getting to New York that they would sing "Trying," a ballad of unrequited love by Billy Vaughn. On the one hand, the suitor "with tears in his eyes" is trying to forget his lost love; on the other, he is trying to get her back. Then he decides to "leave his foolish pride" behind him and "possess her." He knows this probably will not work, but "you can't blame a fellow for trying." The song had climbed to the top of the *Billboard* charts within just a few weeks of its radio introduction in early 1952. The group could sing it, sure, but how they were going to do it was a troublesome question.

They were ushered into a huge CBS rehearsal hall where at

least twenty other groups were practicing for TV appearances, including spots on the Perry Como and Andy Williams shows. They were greeted by a choreographer. As Don McGuire put it, the Hilltoppers didn't know whether a choreographer "cleaned teeth or polished shoes." The present one was Jon Gregory, fresh in from Hollywood, where he had worked on a successful picture, *She's Working Her Way through College.* His self-confidence could sometimes be mistaken for pushiness and even a bit of arrogance. He did teach the Hilltoppers, however, to change places during their performances and to sway back and forth into their movements. (Some reviewers began to call these movements "the Hilltopper strut.") These maneuvers served them well in the years ahead, though when they paid Gregory $25,000 for his lessons, they were not all convinced. They rehearsed with only a piano accompaniment in the background.[7]

Just before the group was led out on to the *Toast of the Town* stage, one of Sullivan's staffers asked, "How are you going to feel in a few seconds with 40 million people watching you?" One of the Hilltoppers became so nervous at this question that he said later, "I nearly lost my water." Out on stage, Sullivan talked to the group for a minute or so. He asked Jimmy about football back at Western Kentucky and Don about basketball. Then they got into their number. They sang "Trying" and bowed and ran offstage to the acclaims of the audience and of Sullivan himself. After just a few seconds the applause brought them back for another bow; still, the looks on their faces were rather gloomy. "Why didn't you smile?" someone asked them later. Sy Spiegelman answered, "If I had smiled, I would have vomited."[8]

Billy Vaughn's sister, Charlotte ("Coogie"), remembers that

she doesn't know how Billy managed the appearance on the Ed Sullivan show "because he was so bashful." Nonetheless, having been blessed by Ed Sullivan, the Hilltoppers had several national TV shows and international appearances ahead of them. On the Monday following the show, a hundred thousand copies of "Trying" were sold.[9]

Back home in Bowling Green, no one was on hand to greet the returning Hilltoppers after their appearance on the Sullivan show, although they had been goodwill ambassadors to hundreds of thousands of people around the world. Several factors accounted for the lack of hometown welcome. Television in 1952 was still in its infancy, and few people, at least by today's standards, owned sets. Also, *Toast of the Town* was "live" on Sunday nights to audiences only in cities such as New York and Boston and larger cities as far south as Louisville. Bowling Green viewers had to wait until the following Wednesday at 9:00 p.m. to see the Hilltoppers perform on WSM-TV out of Nashville. (Bowling Green did not get its own TV affiliate until the early 1960s. Even then, it was ABC, which would not, of course, have shown the Sullivan show.)[10]

But students paid attention to the hometown boys' making it big in New York. "Our dorm, McLean Hall, had one of the few if not the only TVs on campus. The recreation room in the basement of the dorm was packed like sardines to watch the show on the Wednesday night following the Sullivan show on Sunday, not only with dorm residents but students from all over campus. Safety standards regulating room capacity would certainly have been in violation," one student claimed. "Word got out all over the region," says longtime Westerner Lee Robertson. "It was the biggest thing to happen at Western to have our guys to go to New York and sing on the Ed Sullivan show." A local reporter claimed that by being on the Ed Sullivan show, the Hilltoppers went from being the "toast of the town" to "toast of the nation." And, very definitely, "Hilltopper" was now "a year-round word," not dependent on whatever athletic season was in progress.[11]

Billy Vaughn came from Glasgow, Kentucky. At the age of five, suffering from measles, he started fooling around with musical instruments, and within a few years he had mastered several of them. He played flute, piano, ukulele, and saxophone (later he was famous for his "twin" saxophones—he played two at one time). Never in his life, however, did he take any music lessons. It all came to him naturally. He sang, played, and wrote music on every occasion. He and his sister, Coogie, sometimes put on impromptu performances on the streets of Glasgow in return for a nickel or two from passersby. He also began to sing and play for local barbershop quartets. When Billy was about seven, his mother (who played the piano) entered Coogie and him in a contest; he played the uke and Charlotte sang. Their mother told Coogie to pull Billy's ear when their number was finished, for that was the only way he'd leave the stage. They won the contest.[12]

His father, Alvis Radford Vaughn, was not too thrilled when young Billy demonstrated musical talent and intimated that music would be his life. Declaring that music was the life of a "wastrel," he advised Billy to find an occupation that would make him a living. So Billy became a barber, going to a cosmetic school and getting a hairdressing license. "I dreaded going to get a haircut from Billy," his nephew Bobby Biggers said. "It would take him forever, he would talk to everybody that came by . . . about entertaining and performing." He may have been a barber, but it was clear that music was on his mind. He also worked from time to time in a tobacco warehouse.[13]

Billy enlisted in the army when the United States went to war in December 1941. After his discharge just as the war was ending, he enrolled on the GI Bill at Western Kentucky State Teachers College, only thirty miles or so from his home in Glasgow. He majored in music.

The favorite spot for Billy and hundreds of other students was the Goal Post, owned by Hubert and Gladys Greer and located just across the street from Western's Cherry Hall. Students crammed into the Goal Post's nooks and crannies after classes, to eat hamburgers (many times on credit), play the jukebox, and listen to Billy Vaughn and whoever would join him in the songs of the day.

Another local favorite was the Boots and Saddle Club, owned and operated by Bill and Ada Williams. Billy played piano there on Friday and Saturday nights, accompanying the Ace Dinning Orchestra. One night a tall, dark, and slender young fellow ambled into the club (through the back door, some say) and joined Billy and the orchestra in a few songs. He was a junior football player at Western, and his name was Jimmy Sacca. Instantly popular with the crowds, he was invited back for further performances. Jimmy had already begun a singing career of sorts at Western. He had been a singer for the Red and Grey Orchestra at Western, directed by David "Doc" Livingston. "Sacca sang three or four months with me in the Red and Grey. Then I fired him because he wouldn't learn any new songs," Livingston said. He and Sacca remained the best of friends, sharing many laughs about the time Doc "fired" Jimmy.[14]

Billy had written a few country songs and sold some to music companies in California. There was this other song he had written—not "country," not "western," not really anything except what he hoped was a love ballad. Just by chance he had read the word "trying" in a *Billboard* magazine advertisement and thought it would make a good song title. One night after hours at Boots and Saddle Billy showed the song to Jimmy and asked if he could help record it. Jimmy studied the song and concluded that he could help Billy make a go of it.[15]

Over the next few days, at Billy's request, Jimmy looked around campus for someone to join him in a recording of "Trying." Groups frequently gathered at Billy's apartment and sang around the piano. One of the songs, of course, was "Trying." Sacca, Spiegelman, and their friend Pat Mastroleo had previously made up a trio that frequently sang under the windows of girls' dorms, getting a big kick out of singing songs like "I'm Gonna Sit Right Down and Write Myself a Letter." Everybody loved these serenades; sometimes one of the group would tell the girls, "Here's a song we wrote especially for you," to the delighted squeals of the young coeds. Both Pat and another possibility for "Trying," Russ Brown, had so many "other commitments" primarily in various campus activities, that they could not sing the song at any time. Billy had not intended to sing in any recording of "Trying," just accompany it with the piano. With Russ and Pat out, Billy sang.[16]

Another young Westerner at that time was Don McGuire, who came from Hazard, Kentucky. He grew up in a singing family: his mother and father sang in the church choir, and he and his brother, Bobby, performed in barbershop groups, both quartets and choruses. Jimmy asked Don to join the group planning to make a demo of "Trying." "Sure," Don replied. "I haven't made one this week," he wisecracked. Years later he admitted that at that time he did not even know what a demo was. The two seconds it took for him to give an affirmative answer greatly influenced his life and career.[17]

They already had a reel-to-reel tape recorder, purchased by Billy at a cost of around $30. What they didn't have was a quiet place in which to record. Street traffic caused downtown apartments to be unacceptable, classrooms (the college had Saturday classes) and libraries were too uncertain; a student could very well walk in on a recording session and ruin it altogether.[18]

They finally settled on Van Meter Auditorium, right on the top of the hill overlooking Bowling Green. They picked a Saturday in April at 9:00 a.m. to try to do the recording. It appears that they had some help here. Kelly Thompson was the assistant to president Paul Garrett (later Thompson served as president of Western himself). Thompson was almost always the first one on the hill each day, including weekends. His office, like that of President Garrett, was located in Van Meter. In all likelihood, Thompson, who in the years ahead was a most ardent Hilltoppers fan, let the singing group into the auditorium. Besides, it was the only place on campus with a supposedly good-playing piano.[19]

Don McGuire had to skip Professor J. R. Whitmer's physiology class that morning. He told a few fibs the following Monday morning and got away with it.[20]

From nine o'clock until a bit after noon, the group sang away at "Trying." Sacca was the lead vocalist, McGuire sang bass, Spiegelman was the tenor, and Vaughn covered the baritone as well as the piano playing. The piano, however, had a problem. The soft pedal was broken and would not stay down, giving a tone that Vaughn and his cohorts did not like. They enlisted the services of their good friend Bill "Greek" Ploumis, who became a sort of gofer. He got down on the floor and put a book on top of the pedal. He lay with his head on top of that book, which held down the pedal throughout the "excruciating" takes of "Trying." Billy Vaughn later remarked that Ploumis's name should have been on the label of "Trying" to "compensate for [his] contributions."[21]

At long last the boys finished the tape. They were happy enough with it to try to think up a name for their group. They went through numerous possibilities, keeping in mind that there were several other quartets out in public now, vying for attention. Ultimately, they decided on the Hilltoppers. It did, of course, seem an obvious choice.

Western Kentucky is located on top of one of the highest promontories in Bowling Green or, for that matter, in western Kentucky. Known as Fort Albert Sidney Johnston, after the Civil War general whose troops occupied it, the hill offers commanding vistas of surrounding neighborhoods. It is easily the most beautiful campus in all of Kentucky.

Some say the music group took its name from the athletic teams, and this explanation is plausible enough. Western was strong in football and especially in basketball, and the teams were known as the Hilltoppers. Even without this athletic prowess, however, it would have been logical to name the musical group the Hilltoppers simply because of the geographical contours of the place.

Western was not alone in choosing Hilltopper as its name. In a "Hilltopper" context were West Liberty State College in West Virginia; St. Edward's University in Austin, Texas; and Birmingham-Southern College in Alabama. At one time, Marquette University in Michigan was home to the Hilltoppers.

Nor were the Western Kentucky singing Hilltoppers the only group so named. A Hilltopper group in Chicago played for radio station WLS in the 1930s. It featured Howard Black on guitar, Dwayne Wilson on Hawaiian guitar, and Reggie Cross on harmonica. The group played a variety of tunes, all the way from country to gospel.[22] Another Hilltopper group, formed in 1947, became prominent in Fort Wayne, Indiana, when Nancy Lee and the Hilltoppers hit the airwaves, singing and playing songs from pop to classics. Four people were in this band. Sam DeVincent played accordion and bass; Jack Corman played violin; Roy Hanson played banjo, mandolin, and guitar; and Nancy Lee sang. Performing for more than forty years, this Hilltopper group broadcast on WOWO in Fort Wayne, and on TV they starred on the *Old American Barn Dance.* Both of these groups picked "Hilltopper" because they thought the word included music all the way from folk to opera, just as long as it "had a beautiful message and touched the heart strings." The Roan Mountain singing group in Tennessee also called themselves the Hilltoppers, for obvious reasons.[23]

Thus, the group of young men who struggled through "Trying" on that April morning of 1952 in Van Meter Auditorium on Western Kentucky's campus were not alone in calling themselves the Hilltoppers. If they had known about these previous or contemporary groups, they could very well have said, "Well, we're just carrying on a fine tradition." All schools, teams, or musical groups strive to find a name that, in their opinion, best describes them. (Ancient Athenians used silver as their monetary unit because they thought silver described their character; ancient Spartans used iron.) "Hilltoppers" exemplified success (one never hears about "Hillbottomers," or "Hillmiddlers"), overcoming all obstacles, and reaching the top. For Western, "Hilltopper" was geographically correct; Western does sit on top of a hill. Beyond geography, however, the word Hilltopper became a metaphor for "the very best." At least, that is the way the four singing Hilltoppers and thousands of their dedicated fans considered it.

An exhausted quartet sought out a local disc jockey who might listen to their reel-to-reel tape. He was Bill Stamps of WLBJ, who had a program called *Whistling in the Dark* from 10:30 p.m. to midnight. They took the recording to Stamps and talked him into playing it on the air. By midnight Stamps had over a dozen calls from listeners to play it again. "Trying" was born! "One of the best feelings in my life," Don McGuire remarked, "was the first time I heard the group on radio." He and his three companions were overjoyed and awestruck at the enthusiasm with which their song was greeted by neighborhood listeners.[24]

Stamps, who later became the Hilltoppers' manager, was impressed by the nuances, inflections, and feelings that Jimmy Sacca put into the song. Though bemused at the poor quality of the recording, he was overwhelmed by audience support for the song. He decided that the tape was good enough for his former employer, Randall Wood at Dot Records, down in Gallatin, Tennessee, some forty miles from Bowling Green, to hear.

When Wood, a native of McMinnville, Tennessee, got out of the armed forces in the mid-1940s, he started an electrical appliance store in Gallatin. More or less as a sideline, he stocked classical music records along with a supply of pop music. Many of his customers asked for rhythm and blues records, but they were largely unavailable in Gallatin. He advertised for rhythm and blues 78 rpm records in Nashville, and the results were gratifying. He began what ultimately proved to be a lucrative 78 R & B mail-order business, and he changed the name of his establishment to Randy's Record Shop. Before long he could claim to be the largest retailer of records east of the Mississippi.[25]

It seemed natural for him ultimately to get into the recording business himself. He and a business partner, Beasley Smith of Nashville (about twenty-five miles west of Gallatin), opened Dot Records. Smith, originally from McEwan, Tennessee, was a well-known Nashville orchestra conductor in the 1920s, becoming in 1935 the musical conductor for radio station WSM.

Wood decided to take a chance on this singing group at WKSC just up the road a ways from Gallatin. He and Al Bennett (who later became vice president of Dot Records) began to make arrangements for the Hilltoppers first real recording session. Certainly his sound equipment was better than the cheap recorder the boys had used before. The only musical instrument at the session was the ever-present piano (later, at the Gallatin studio, a bass violin was dubbed in).

The best place for this second recording was once again Van Meter Auditorium. Its cavernous features gave the stage a stereo sound. And they felt that Van Meter presented the best opportunity for privacy. In fact, their plans were kept under wraps for several days; only a few insiders were privy to them.

This second recording was in May 1952, again on a Saturday. They were going to start this time, however, at 6:00 p.m. rather than 9:00 a.m. There had been no basketball or baseball games that day, so the chances of noisy students interrupting their performance were at a minimum. The only problem, as it had been before, was how to gain entry into the huge auditorium. Not even Kelly Thompson was around on early Saturday evenings.

The lone campus policeman, Aubrey Hoofnel, was, though. He was strictly a law-and-order and by-the-book man. He carried a pistol and on more than one occasion had threatened to use it against a student or other "troublemaker." The Hilltoppers were afraid of him, but they worked up enough nerve to offer him $10 if he would unlock the doors to Van Meter, and give them some privacy for the next several hours. He accepted their offer.

Some eight to ten friends accompanied the Hilltoppers, Wood, and Bennett into the auditorium. Years later, Don McGuire chuckled, "at least a quarter of a million people have claimed to be at that session."[26]

At the end of each take, Don and his compatriots would pronounce it "perfect." Wood, however, was hard to please. It took six hours and thirty takes for him even to begin to nod agreement. When the group finished with what they thought was the final take of "Trying," Wood smilingly told them, "Now we have to have a backside." They sang "You Made Up My Mind," and Wood was pleased with it. *"But,"* he said ominously, "we need to do another take of 'Trying.'" Keeping their groans to themselves, The Hilltoppers sang it one more time. When it was finished, they were reassured by the big smile on Randy's face. "That's the take," he proclaimed. "We'll put the record out." The ending of this particular take was the worst one, in the opinion of the vocalists. "That was the genius of the man," McGuire admiringly remembered. The group never again questioned Wood's strategy and direction. He released the record to the public on May 25, 1952, and it certainly did change a lot of lives. Dot 15018 became Randy's Record Shop's first pop-chart hit.[27]

The month after the second Van Meter recording, the Hilltoppers were guests on *Carousel,* a live TV show originating on WSM in Nashville. Another Music City offering, *Tin Pan Alley,* on NBC, also invited the Hilltoppers to perform. Of course "Trying" was always at the top of their repertoire. They were interviewed via telephone by a disc jockey in Buffalo, New York. *And* they enrolled in summer school at Western.[28]

"Trying" shot up in every chart in America, and then, inexplicably, by fall 1952, it precipitously dropped off, though it was still popular, as one might imagine, in Bowling Green and to a lesser extent in Nashville. Wood called the Hilltoppers together at his Gallatin office for a strategy session, to try to get them interested in other material. "Trying" just doesn't seem to be making it, was Wood's message to the young students from Western Kentucky. "Their spirits," as *Louisville Courier-Journal* columnist Joe Creason colorfully put it, "were lower than a well digger's instep." Sacca began to doubt his and his friends' futures in the recording industry, but he was buoyed up by Wood's promise of additional engagements. Wood was not going to abandon them, for he thought the Hilltoppers were the "greatest" singing group "to ever hit the market."[29]

While they were in Wood's office that day, the telephone rang. An excited secretary ran in to tell Wood that the Dot distributor in Cincinnati, Izzy Nathan, was on the line. Record buyers and disc jockeys all over the area were calling for the song. A few minutes later, Art Freeman, the Dot distributor in Cleveland, telephoned with essentially the same message. Fans wanted recordings of "Trying," and they couldn't get them fast enough.

By early August "Trying" was twenty-ninth on the *Billboard* popularity chart. It was a best seller in Pittsburgh, number four in Chicago, among the top five in New York, Louisville, and New Orleans. Nationwide, it jumped to number ten. Other artists began to record "Trying." They included Johnny Desmond, Jimmy Palmer, Todd Rhodes, Grady Martin, Ralley Hefferson and the Brigadiers, and of most significance, sentimentally at least, the one and only Ella Fitzgerald. The Hilltoppers' recording of "Trying" altogether sold almost a million copies.[30]

Coincidence? No, said Jimmy Sacca. "Everything is fate." He added, "It had to be. How else can you explain how a kid like me . . . could find his way to Western Kentucky, meet three other guys, and end up on the Ed Sullivan show, almost overnight?" Providential?[31]

Whatever it was, it worked. Both Freeman and Nathan told Wood that "Trying" was "going off the charts" in their cities and was undoubtedly going to be a hit. They did not have enough copies, however, to meet customer demand. Randy Wood sent each distributor some ten thousand records and sat back and waited for results. One thing was clear: the Hilltoppers were on their way.

And the first thing about "being on their way" was the Ed

Sullivan show. The telephone calls from Cincinnati and Cleveland came in on a Wednesday morning. The very next day, Thursday, the Ed Sullivan show called with a "command performance" type of inquiry, wanting to know if the Hilltoppers were available for the following Sunday night. Yes they were, and this is where the Buick comes into the picture, as well as last-minute, almost frantic discussions about what to wear.[32]

White buckskin shoes, or, as teens knew them, "white bucks"—just like Pat Boone's—were popular in the early fifties, so there was no problem here. What kind of shirt, though? Jimmy and Don had lettered at Western, so they were entitled to wear the big W. But when Sullivan beckoned, Jimmy couldn't find his own, and after some persuasion, his friend Warren Mahan lent him his letter sweater. Mahan remarked later, "After I exacted a pledge on his life that it would be returned, I never saw it again." Billy, who had been a student at Western, and Seymour, who was majoring in music, wore the W along with Jimmy and Don as a part of the Hilltopper costume. (Possibly one reason Mahan never saw his sweater again was that when the boys got to CBS, a Sullivan functionary feared that their red sweaters with gray letters "would not show up well on black-and-white TV." So, because of the "primitive nature" of early television broadcasts, each boy had to purchase a maroon sweater with an off-white W. Wearing the original red sweaters with the W, said local sports-store owner Herman Lowe, was his idea. The group came to his store and asked him for suggestions about what uniform to wear. Then the subject, according to Lowe, turned to what they would wear on their heads. It was Billy, primarily, who wanted something to cover his balding spots. "The [other three] boys, with fine heads of hair, didn't think too well of the idea," but "we settled for a skull cap in Western colors."[33]

For some time, their clothes—flannel pants, beanies, and sweaters with a large W on them—were the Hilltoppers' trademark, just as "Trying" became their signature song. After the calls from Cincinnati and Cleveland and their appearance on the Ed Sullivan show, offers for performances poured in. Of course, their paychecks increased considerably; still, they were mindful of expenses. When they performed at a Pittsburgh nightclub, for example, they slept on their friend Bill Ploumis's floor.[34]

These Ed Sullivan veterans were still in college during the heady days when they were performing at Moe's Main Street in Cleveland and at spots in Philadelphia, Akron, Toledo, and other cities. They'd leave on a late Friday afternoon flight out of Bowling Green, always piloted by Wilbur Parrish, perform Friday, Saturday, and Sunday nights, and return in the wee hours of Monday for classes. Coming back after a weekend trip, Jimmy, Don, and Seymour would "dash to boarding house rooms, gaze longingly at their beds, grab loads of textbooks and run up the hill to Western Kentucky State College." On one occasion, it was reported, when the group left Yonkers, New York, after a concert, a group of fans followed them to the plane. The last words the fans heard came from Seymour: "Hey, you guys, has anybody seen my French book?"[35]

So, when Jimmy, Don, and Seymour sat down at their desks at the start of the week and someone would invariably ask them, "How was your weekend?" they could very well proclaim, "I was in Boston," or Baltimore, or anywhere they had been performing during that time. "There are students at Western," wrote Creason, "who sit in the same classes with them who aren't aware that they're splitting infinitives and doing math problems with musical hotshots."[36]

Why didn't they just quit college and record top-of-the-chart hits? Despite all their efforts to be on time, they did miss an unusual number of classes, and they, as Jimmy Sacca attests, did not perform "brilliantly" in academics.

It is often asserted that some groups experience "overnight" success only after many years of struggle and effort, giving the appearance of instant success. With the Hilltoppers, however, success really came overnight. In early 1952, the four might have known each other in casual ways. They could join in a barbershop rendition or sing under coeds' windows. Who could have predicted, that before the end of 1952, they would be joined together as a group, singing "Trying," and getting ready to go on to worldwide fame?

The Korean War had started in June 1950, and it influenced the lives of tens of thousands of young men around the country. If they stayed in college, they were draft exempt. Get out, and away they went into the armed forces. The Hilltoppers, therefore, had good reasons for staying in school.

One of their most beloved and respected recordings was a later song entitled "Time Waits for No One." This could very well have become their theme song in late 1952 as graduation dates and "greetings" from Uncle Sam loomed.

2 A Gathering of the Hilltoppers

In 1952, Bowling Green, Kentucky, was a sleepy little college town with some twenty thousand residents. Added to this number were the sixteen hundred or so students who attended Western Kentucky State College on top of the big hill.[1]

As one might imagine, most students came to Western primarily because it was far enough *from* home for an eighteen-year-old to experience some independence. Second, it was close enough *to* home to get the weekly laundry done by Mother. Overwhelmingly, students came from south-central Kentucky: Warren, Barren, Butler, Edmonton, Ohio, Grayson, Simpson, and Logan counties. Students from farther afield in Kentucky, except perhaps for Louisville, were fairly much anomalies. Occasionally, there were enrollments from nearby Tennessee and a few now and then from Indiana and even Pennsylvania (which was a good football breeding ground). Out-of-state enrollment was picking up by the early 1950s, but Western was overwhelmingly dominated by native-born Kentuckians.

Billy Vaughn came to Western because it was practically in his backyard. Glasgow, just thirty miles north of Bowling Green, was a natural source for WKSC students. Don McGuire, like Vaughn a Kentucky boy, came from relatively faraway Hazard, but, as already noted, basketball brought him to Western.

Seymour Spiegelman hailed from historic Seneca Falls, New York. How could he find himself among a set of people with strange accents, many of whom looked upon him as some kind of alien from outer space?

Though neither of his parents played or sang, they encouraged Seymour and his sister, Shirley, to join high school glee clubs and choruses. Their father, Jacob (usually called Jack), died in 1946, leaving their mother, Yetta Pearl, with limited financial resources. Seymour was a student at Fredonia College in upstate New York at his father's death and found it increasingly difficult to afford school. Therefore, he began to apply around the country for musical scholarships. A little college in Kentucky gave him his chance. He came to Western Kentucky and majored in music, becoming upon graduation a certified teacher.[2]

And then, there was Jimmy Sacca. Lockport, New York, is not far from Spiegelman's hometown of Seneca Falls, but Jimmy and Sy did not know each other until they got to Kentucky. Throughout his years at Eastman High School in Lockport, Jimmy had starring parts in operas and solos in choir. His great idol was, and is, Frank Sinatra: "I breathe when he breathes. I listen to him for hours."[3]

One of Jimmy's good friends at Eastman, Joe Montedoro, was on the football team. The coach, Hopper Kennedy, knew Western Kentucky's football coach, Jack Clayton, and offered to help Joe get a scholarship. When Joe planned to travel to Bowling Green in 1949 to try out for football, it occurred to him that he faced a grueling twenty-four-hour bus ride. Not wanting to undertake such an odyssey alone, Joe asked Jimmy Sacca to go with him. Jimmy agreed. The two friends, dusty and exhausted, finally arrived in the Bluegrass state.[4]

Joe reported immediately to Coach Clayton, who told him that scrimmage hours (since classes had not yet started) were from 9:00 a.m. to noon each day, and then again from 2:00 to 5:00 p.m. So for six hours each day, Jimmy was left to his own devices. "I was there all by myself. I was bored," he recalled. Then Jimmy decided to go to the practice sessions himself. Even if he didn't like them, they would be better than lounging around all day, not really having anything to do.[5]

Coach Clayton liked what he saw. Jimmy could pass a ball as well as catch it, and he was a fine runner. Joe finally completed his tryouts for the football team, and he and Jimmy bade farewell to Coach Clayton and their fellow players. The coach promised to get in touch. True to his word, Clayton wrote, promising a football scholarship, not to Joe Montedoro, but to Jimmy Sacca. "I decided to come here and try it," Jimmy said. He hopped a Greyhound back to Bowling Green, to continue practicing with the football team.[6]

He didn't know anybody. He was now in a school where most students, to his ear at least, spoke with outlandish accents, and he was certainly regarded by the largely southern student body as a novelty with his own strange way of speaking. He suffered homesickness, just as any young person would have done. He longed for his parents, who were in the produce business back in Lockport, and sometimes felt so forlorn that he lay in his bed and cried. One of his teammates, Max Stevens, took Jimmy under his wing and began to "show him the town." As a result, Jimmy said, somewhat mysteriously, "After that, I didn't even want to go home."[7]

So, two New Yorkers teamed up with two Kentuckians on the campus of Western Kentucky State College to become the

Hilltoppers. In a way, this union symbolized a coming together of North and South, a notion that one should put aside sectional differences and concentrate on similarities. How fitting that it was Kentucky where these four young men came together. Even geographically, Kentucky is a compromise. It is between the North and the South of the United States and, for that matter, between the East and the West. [8]

Hilltopper music created a unity that evolved from local interest to national significance. It was not that long a time from the Sullivan show on October 26, 1952, to early 1953, when the Hilltoppers recorded a Johnny Mercer song, "P.S. I Love You," once again for Dot Records. (This song had been recorded earlier by Rudy Vallee, Eddie Stone, and Will Osborne.) The Hilltoppers had already been blessed with numerous theater and nightclub appearances after their spot on the Sullivan show, and then "P.S. I Love You" became a gold record, selling over a million copies. By June 1953, "P.S." was number six in Pittsburgh and St. Louis and number sixteen on jukeboxes throughout the country. By July it was number five among the records "most played by jockeys" in the United States, and at the end of the year it had hit the *Billboard*'s Honor Roll of Hits and received every other honor possible.[9]

"P.S. I Love You" is about two lovers who have been separated by circumstance. The one left behind wants to know how the trip went. He hopes everything is fine and then says that he has burned a hole in the dining room table. It looks like rain, he says, but he can't "complain." After these mundane things had been mentioned the lover almost absent-mindedly writes, "P.S. I love you."

This song exemplified the mood of American life in early

1953. Many young men had gone off to the Korean War in the previous two years, and as a result many real-life love letters had been written. Parents, siblings, and above all sweethearts wanted to tell their absent men about the doings in their hometowns and communities. To make sure that their sentiments were rightly expressed and understood, it was not unusual for them to add to their letters "P.S. I love you." It was somewhat equivalent to SWAK (Sealed with a kiss) in World War II, or SVBEV in Roman times, which stood for "Si vales bene est, valeo"—"If you are well, so am I").

Seymour Spiegelman's daughter Penelope (Penny) has always held "P.S. I Love You" as her favorite Hilltopper tune. Her father told her that the song meant "Penny Spiegelman, I Love You." (He also told his young daughter that Perry Como sang "Pennies from Heaven" just for her.) Her father's voice, she said, "was booming, and it took a lot of control on his part to stay blended and not drown everyone else out." He took such great joy in singing that it went from "the bottom of his feet to the top of his head." His other daughter, Suellyn, admiringly asserted that Seymour "was such an incredible, kind, funny man who had a passion for life. . . . Singing with the Hilltoppers was such a thrill for him." Sy sang with the choir at the Methodist church in Moulton, Alabama, hometown of his wife, Jeannie Warren, as well as at the local synagogue on high holy days.[10]

The flip side of "P.S. I Love You" was "I'd Rather Die Young." In a way, this choice was as much strategic as artistic. Most northern disc jockeys would not play a song with the word "die" in it. Many southern disc jockeys, however, viewed "I'd Rather Die Young" as the heart of country music, and it became popular south of the Mason-Dixon Line. To pair "I'd

Rather Die Young" with a song on its way to stardom assured its ultimate success. Once listeners got beyond the first few lines of the song, they loved it, both in the North and in the South. It is a love song about one lover desperate to keep the other from leaving; it became a trademark of the Hilltoppers' growing fame. As sung by the group, the emotional impact of Jimmy's singing, the soft piano sweeps by Billy, and the contributions of the boys in the background is quite striking. Who could resist such a ballad?[11]

By mid-1953 the Hilltoppers were nationally and internationally known. Their ascendancy had been breathtakingly swift. Of course, they were not alone. Several quartets had hit the scene in the late 1940s and early 1950s, including the Platters (at one point a quintet), the Four Aces, the Four Lads, and the Four Freshmen.

Because the Platters (whose rendition of "The Great Pretender" was frequently compared to the Hilltoppers' version of "The Joker") were black, their music was usually billed in the late fifties and early sixties as rock 'n' roll. Disc jockey Alan Freed has usually been credited with coining the phrase "rock n roll" in 1955; in 1952–1953 the Platters were known widely as "rhythm and blues" and "pop." The Platters made the sound track for Bill Haley's movie, *Rock Around the Clock.* One Hilltopper fan, Patsy Cusham of Northumberland, England, wrote, "We boo-ed when The Platters sang it [the sound track]" instead of the Hilltoppers. "You should have heard the row" at the cinema because the Hilltoppers had not been chosen, she said.[12]

The Platters became famous for "Only You," written by their producer, Buck Ram, and also recorded by the Ink Spots and the Hilltoppers; "My Prayer," "The Magic Touch," "You'll Never, Never Know," and "I've Been Thinking." Lead singer Tony Williams had a "pleasing style" of singing, to the "fine accompaniment" of his background colleagues.[13]

The Four Aces performed the sound track for the tender movie *Love Is a Many Splendored Thing,* starring Jennifer Jones and William Holden. The group's rendition of "Three Coins in a Fountain" in the early 1950s was popular throughout the world. Al Alberts was the Four Aces lead singer, and he performed "brilliant solo efforts" backed up with "bouncy rhythms."

The Four Lads were young Canadians, so, unlike the Hilltoppers, they did not have to worry about the draft that applied in the United States when the Korean War started. They could and did come and go in the States as they pleased. Their song "Moments to Remember" caught on with the listening public in both the United States and Great Britain, as did, at least to some extent, their versions of "I've Been Thinking," and "Standing on the Corner."

Another group from the 1950s (still going in the early twenty-first century with, of course, different members from the originals) that may be compared and put into the context of the career of the singing Hilltoppers was the Four Freshmen, out of Butler University in Indianapolis. One music fan said that the Four Freshmen always sounded "very rehearsed, smooth, with the touch of a big band. . . . I can't see them as individuals" as he could with the Hilltoppers. Some listeners placed the Four Freshmen in the genre of progressive jazz. According to one fan, the Four Freshmen's lead singer, Bobby Flanagan, tried too hard to "be hip," when he really didn't know how to be.

"There's just not much love in his music," this correspondent argued. Flanagan and his group, he said, were too full of ego. "If he [Flanagan] were singing 'P.S. I Love You,' it would be more like 'P.S. I Love Myself.'"[14]

There were, of course, many other black and white male quartets at the time, most of them brought up in barbershop harmony and country music styles. Their performances marked a transition from the era of big bands to rock 'n' roll. The Hilltoppers did not copy any other groups, black or white, nor were their individual sounds "used as a blueprint by any early rock and roll groups." Thus, they were unique in the musical world of the 1950s. Billy Vaughn, the founding father of the Hilltoppers, was identified with barbershop and country, and only when the Hilltoppers began full-time performing did they become known for their love ballads.[15]

The rise of male quartets in the early 1950s may be attributed in part to the enactment in many cities of "cabaret laws," which tended to work against the large jazz bands of the late 1940s. These cabaret laws dated back to the late 1920s, when the jazz age was in full swing. Many large urban governments, including New York City, citing moral and noise considerations, placed limits on how many instruments a band could bring for a performance at a nightclub or other entertainment establishment. When the big jazz bands were discouraged, the doors were opened for smaller groups to become major entertainers.[16]

Factors other than cabaret laws also have to be considered in the decline of the big bands. A musicians' strike in 1948 cut into the number of big band performances; costs of transporting large numbers of musicians rose because of the discontinuance of price controls after World War II; and of course, consumer tastes were changing. Music is as subject to "cyclical vogues" as any other form of art. Disseminated by the mass media—radio, records, and, in the late forties and early fifties, television—music is never static; it is always in motion, always evolving. Though for several months, the Hilltoppers performed more for the jukebox and the recording industry than in live performances, they nevertheless, like members of other quartets, benefited from the cabaret laws.[17]

The great difference between groups such as the Platters, the Four Lads, and the Hilltoppers is that the Hilltoppers had the incredible singing voice of Jimmy Sacca. Italians are well known for their operatic abilities, and Jimmy Sacca could, as one admiring fan said, just as easily have gone into grand opera as join a quartet. Jimmy's voice "was beautifully natural, vibrant, and emotional. There was nothing faky or faddish about it." Another fan asserted that "Jimmy's voice was unique. It touched almost everyone who heard him sing. I have 1000s of songs of many artists; I am yet to hear one that sounds like Jimmy Sacca." What was it about Jimmy Sacca's voice that caused people, critics and fans alike, to remark so many times on its uniqueness?[18]

When Jimmy sang, he had a follow-through. He would finish a line or phrase of a song and then give an explosive "hehhh," "ehhh," "hahhh," or "huhhh" to it. These additives, or aspirations, went on longer in some songs than others. They were a way of "hanging" the last word of a line. Writer Wayne Stierle reported that "at the end of a phrase," Jimmy pushed an "extra breath into the word." On the word "mine," for example, closing a phrase, "it would become, 'mine. . .' (slight pause holding) . . . eh; mine-eh.'"[19]Jimmy said he was unaware of putting anything special into his style of singing. That was just his way, in the manner of Italian opera singers. (One can hear Luciano Pavarotti do the same thing in grand opera.) His style attracted the attention of many reviewers of the day, who classified it in varying ways, from an "echo chamber" to "open-air" singing. Jimmy's sound was distinctive, as an observer noted, a sort of "struggle and release," building up a line of music until "it exploded."[20]

One English reviewer did not particularly like Jimmy's "escape clauses." Simon Ward, writing for the *Daily Sketch,* said that Jimmy's final "explosions" of phrases and consonants with distinctive vowel sounds were "un-necessary." Only too happy to get in a dig at England's cross-Channel neighbor, Ward wrote that Jimmy's style was "in the manner of reciting French poetry."[21]

It could well be that Jimmy was influenced here by Billy Vaughn himself, who, in addition to being a Hilltopper, began to arrange music for Dot Records in Gallatin. He had many clients who became famous, including Pat Boone. Boone recorded "April Love" in Dot's studio, but it "needed something." It should be "more dramatic." Therefore, Billy wrote the nonsense phrase, "ba ba ba ba ba bah" into the second part of the song. This actually caught on with the American jukebox audience, and "April Love" became a million-plus seller. Pat Boone attributes much of his musical success to Hilltopper Billy Vaughn.[22]

It is almost certain that Jimmy Sacca did not realize that his way of singing probably reminded many southern audiences of going to church. Old-time southern preachers had a way of working themselves into frenzies when they delivered their messages. Frequently at the end of a sentence, a preacher would fervently add vowel sounds such as "ahhh," "ehhh," "uhhh," and other hanging effects to his presentation. In all likelihood, the "preacher effect" of Jimmy Sacca's singing influenced the good citizens of Bowling Green, Nashville, and points south.

And, on into 1953, their jukebox career flourished. "P.S. I Love You" continued to be a favorite of the "invisible" or "silent" generation, the teens and young adults of the first Eisenhower administration. They did not attend very many live performances, preferring to go to a café and listen to a jukebox. The jukebox became so popular with this generation that establishments sometimes put "mini-jukeboxes" on the walls at each booth. Just put in a nickel, and music of your favorite singing group (in many instances, the Hilltoppers) would soon permeate the place. "I'd Rather Die Young," the B side of "P.S. I Love You," ran up very high ratings on jukeboxes. "Love Walked In" climbed to number four in Pittsburgh, number nine in Seattle and Cincinnati, nine in New York, and four in New Orleans. The Hilltoppers were now in the top echelon of American singing groups. They certainly shared in comedian Jackie Gleason's cry of triumph: "How sweet it is!" The Hilltoppers and other pop bands, and their audiences, could use the jukebox to escape the major political concerns of the day, which included the "red-baiting" tactics of Senator Joseph McCarthy of Wisconsin. The best way to offset this kind of xenophobia and bigotry was just to keep singing. As the old saying goes, "How many people have you ever seen afightin' when they were singin' a song?" And that's what the Hilltoppers did: they kept right on singing.[23]

Another reason that young people did not favor live performances was the rise of television in the 1950s. They could stay at home and have front-row seats to some of the world's greatest musical performances. This was the first generation of Americans to be raised on TV, giving society the "wild, moody, rebellious, soulful, and idealistic creature we know as the American teenager." The pop music of that era formed teenagers' identity. They wanted music "that spoke to their own condition," including themes of first love, "fights with parents," frustration with high school, and difficulties with the "older generation." In every age, "adolescents find a style of music that expresses some of the yearning, the frustrations, and the frantic searching quality that young people have." The 1950s, some authors asserted, "essentially invented the teenager as a commercial and cultural entity."[24]

The Hilltoppers took their place in the panoply of singing and other musical groups in the early to middle part of the decade. The Hilltoppers, of course, had to compete with other singing groups and get onto *Billboard* and other charts. Here they were quite successful, as seen by their *Billboard* ratings over the years.

Although they were most popular among the jukebox crowd, and held their own on radio and television, the Hilltoppers also made personal appearances. They traveled far and wide while still students at Western Kentucky State College. One trip was to Kansas City, Missouri, after which they had an engagement in St. Louis, directly across the state. As they were driving east toward St. Louis, a police car pulled in behind them with red lights flashing and sirens wailing. "We pulled over," recalled Don McGuire. "Sir, we are an entertainment group," the four explained; still, they had to put their hands on top of the car and plead with the officer—who had his gun out the whole time—to let them produce the contract for their next performance and thus demonstrate that they were peaceful citizens. There had been a bank robbery earlier that day in Kansas City, the trooper told them, by four men riding in a car very similar to theirs. They finally convinced the highway patrolman of their innocence and were allowed to continue their trip to St. Louis.[25]

Their troubles, however, were not yet over. The gas gauge read empty, and by now it was late at night, and all the filling stations were closed. For the next seventy-five miles, they had to stop at thirty or so different closed stations and drain the hoses to get the gas left behind by the last customers of the day. By hopscotching from one station to another, they finally got to St. Louis, where they performed at Casey's Nightclub.[26]

Once, when the Hilltoppers were in New York, going in a taxi to their hotel after an engagement, they passed by a subway station. Billy Vaughn, trying to act the Kentucky hillbilly, asked, "How do they get the trains down there?"

Sy Spiegelman, always with a ready riposte, replied, "Do you see those handrails there at the stairs going down?"

Billy answered, "Yes."

"Well," Sy replied, "they put the trains on those railings and roll them down to the subway, so they can then use them for passengers."

"Oh, I see," Billy answered in all innocence.[27]

By this time, the New York cabbie was convulsed with laughter.

Billy liked to play practical jokes, especially during rehearsal sessions. Once, when the group was trying to learn a new song and had to hold the sheet music in front of them, Billy slipped up and with a cigarette lighter set fire to the pages. To this day, Don McGuire does not remember the name of the song they were rehearsing. Sometimes, if Don or another singer began to sing either too low or too high, Billy would run up behind them and give them a big goose under their arms or on some other part of their anatomy and then run around the stage showing the audience his thumb. He also loved to "eat" cigarettes during recording sessions. He would put a mostly smoked cigarette into his mouth and pretend to devour it. Of course, he had saved up quite a bit of saliva for the occasion. These were, to be sure, gimmicks, and the audiences loved them.[28]

Despite their huge successes, these four young men kept things in perspective. They may have attained fame in only a year or so, but they still were, as one journal reported, "teenagers at heart." After they had checked into one hotel while on the road, the desk clerk remarked, "Those four singer chaps are quite refined gentlemen." At the very moment he uttered these words, three of the four were "pounding each other in a knock-down, drag-'em-out pillow fight" in their room. The fourth was telephoning the hotel's drugstore, asking that chocolate malts be sent up. These kids, "known only to their college profs" a few months before, were now becoming familiar to music-loving crowds throughout the nation and, indeed, the world.[29]

Of course, they had fun on the road, but they had even more fun back at campus. They kept up a semblance of study. (There is a photo of Jimmy Sacca and his songmates studying in the library. Jimmy says this picture was "posed.") They were greeted on campus as a "famous singing group" who had brought "honor" and "respect" to the Western campus. They also practiced fairly regularly, using Professor Bennie Beach's studio in the old (1936) music building, which had a piano in one of its big rooms. Sometimes Don and Billy livened up these practice sessions with a "torrid variety of Two-on-a-Piano work."[30]

As is well known, fame invites imitation, and the Hilltoppers were no exception. Some of the Hilltoppers' best friends formed a group called the Hillfloppers to parody the real group. William "Whitey" Sanders (who went on to become a famous newspaper cartoonist) played guitar, Joe Hardy the homemade drums, and Warren Mahan the washtub bass. The Hillfloppers played once for a dance at University High School (the old teacher training institution at Western). They also performed in dormitory lobbies (especially in women's dorms) and occasionally at one of Bowling Green's numerous beer joints. [31]

Then there was the famous water-pouring incident, which for years was attributed to one of the singing Hilltoppers. On a late spring day in the early 1950s (accounts vary), the famous tenor Jan Peerce came to Western to perform at Van Meter Auditorium, very close to Potter Hall, where the Hilltoppers lived. During the Peerce concert, apparently someone in Potter, taking a long, comforting shower, began singing at the top of his voice, "Give Me That Old Mountain Dew," much to the chagrin of the tenor and, as it turned out, to the displeasure of Western's dean of faculties, Dr. Finley Grise.[32]

Warren Mahan of the Hillfloppers was about to leave his room when he heard from Whitey Sanders that they had an engagement that night for a jam session at a local cafeteria. Well, they needed some practice, right? They started playing, quite loudly, and many members of the audience at Van Meter (who had been forced there in the first place by their teachers) started hanging out the windows listening to what was going on at Potter, in effect ignoring the famous tenor. (The weather was warm and this was well before any building at Western was air-conditioned.)

Knotty McFadden was on the third floor of Potter Hall, overlooking the patio, where the Hillfloppers were practicing for their performance. McFadden "was notorious for dumping water on our housemother, Pearl Rutledge, as she sun-bathed on the Potter Hall back patio."[33]

So, according to Warren Mahan, it was McFadden who threw the water that day, apparently aiming for the Hillfloppers. Unfortunately, Dean Grise appeared at the same time as the water was thrown. "As the Dean arrived on the scene, Knotty hit him with the full load of the water." The dean was "red-faced, sputtering," and totally "enraged" as he stalked back to Van Meter, while Mahan and McFadden beat it out of Potter, over an embankment to the nearest street. No one ever said whether the Peerce performance went on to a successful finale.[34]

It was widely thought throughout the campus (and probably by Dean Grise himself) that the culprit was Jimmy Sacca. Only now, over a half century later, the truth is known. One can only wish to have seen the good dean in all his dampened glory.

Why Jimmy? Apparently like a rather large number of students at Western at the time, Jimmy had a history with the dean. Apparently, the dean did not mind Jimmy's affiliation with the Hilltoppers as they appeared on the national scene. But between engagements, Jimmy and his three colleagues sometimes indulged in "extracurricular" activities. For example, Jimmy sang from time to time at a Bowling Green nightclub named Manhattan Towers at the end of College Street, just by the bridge across the Barren River, "surrounded on three sides by a cow pasture." There was nothing wrong in that, of course, but many good citizens of Bowling Green considered performing at *any* nightclub to be disreputable.[35]

Rumors kept floating around town about the "rowdy" nature of Manhattan Towers. One of Jimmy's friends was a waiter at the establishment, as was Jimmy during the week. According to reports, one night the waiter was taking a large tray of ice to a table when much of it spilled over into the rather low-cut blouse of a lady in attendance. Without thinking too much about it, the waiter immediately set about trying to get the ice out of the woman's bosom. One witness said wryly, "She hated the ice," but not, apparently, its retrieval.[36]

Jimmy's football career at Western ended rather abruptly because of an incident when the team was on its way to Florida. The players stopped overnight at an Atlanta hotel and were warned by their coaches, at the risk of being expelled from the team, not to break curfew. Jimmy learned that famed percussionist Gene Krupa was performing that night no more than two blocks away from the hotel, and he could not resist this opportunity. Jimmy went down the fire escape and saw the show. When it ended, the hour was late, so Jimmy walked boldly into the hotel's main lobby—and into the arms of a waiting coach. Unfortunately for Jimmy, the coaching staff had conducted a bed check, and found Jimmy missing. They predicted he would come back not via the fire escape but through the main lobby. They were correct.[37]

After he had quit football, Jimmy became a member of the Western Kentucky marching band, playing the clarinet. At a game with Murray, a serious altercation occurred between the bands from the two schools. Jimmy started off the field, either to observe or participate. The band director told him he could not participate in hostilities of any sort in a band uniform, so Jimmy ripped off his band jacket, which had two rows of buttons on each side, and headed for the confrontation. According to one witness, Jimmy "hit a guy" from Murray with his clarinet. Jimmy—who remembers this event as being at Eastern Kentucky State College—said that he was defending his old friend Bill "the Greek" Ploumis, who had been assaulted by two band members from the other team. It was "by instinct" that Jimmy took off his hat and jacket and helped Ploumis. Jimmy's instincts, though, were not amusing to the band director, Hugh Gunderson, who fired him once they got back to campus. These incidents–breaking curfew in Atlanta and fisticuffs at the stadium—did not escape the attention of Western's chief academic officer.[38]

Even the appearance of irregularities was enough to set off Dean Grise. Jimmy and the Hilltoppers had become known far and wide as "serenaders" on the campus, particularly late at night at girls' dormitories. Jimmy was also in some of the plays and musicals put on by the theater department. In *Moon over Miami* Jimmy performed several musical numbers. Apparently the dean attended one of the performances and, for reasons he never made clear, was upset with Jimmy's songs. Dean Grise called Jimmy into his office and told him to report to the president, Dr. Paul Garrett, to explain himself. Jimmy presented himself to President Garrett, who looked at him seriously for a minute or two. Then he told the young performer, "'Moon over Miami' is my favorite song." The president wanted Jimmy to stand there before him in his office at Van Meter and sing the song a cappella. Jimmy sang "Moon over Miami" for an audience of one: President Paul Garrett. When Jimmy finished the song, President Garrett said, "Yes, young man, that's my favorite song. Thank you, and now get the hell out of my office." That was the end of Jimmy's troubles with Dean Grise.[39]

Then there was the time that Whitey Sanders "hypnotized" Jimmy to keep him from smoking in a crowded automobile. Whitey, Jimmy, and four compadres were driving to Louisville to watch a basketball game. Around Elizabethtown, Jimmy, sitting in the front on the passenger side, lit up what he considered to be a badly needed cigarette. It was too cold to roll down the windows and too warm to tolerate the smoke. His friends insisted that he extinguish the cigarette, which he grudgingly did. Then he went to sleep. While Jimmy slept, Whitey talked to him in a monotone, telling him that the next cigarette he lit up would taste like an old rubber tire. Pulling into Louisville, Jimmy lit up and started hacking and coughing. "He demanded to know what we had done to his cigarettes while he was asleep," Sanders recounted. Sanders finally told Jimmy that he had been hypnotized. "By early evening, the suggestion had worn off [but] I suspect to this day that he still does not believe what happened."[40]

By early 1953 Jimmy Sacca and his Hilltopper brethren knew that soon they would have to make some basic decisions. It was just a matter of time until one or more of them would be drafted into the military services, even though the war in Korea at this time was entering its final phase. (The armistice was signed on July 27, 1953, a bit over four months after Jimmy entered the service.) The group began to record more songs than usual, anticipating the draft, hoping that the Hilltoppers would stay alive in the jukeboxes, if not at public performances. They began to realize that the original group—the ones who had caused so much commotion on campus in the first place—would probably have to go through the painful process of losing members and seeing them replaced by someone else.

Later, in 1955, while Jimmy was still in the army, Billy Vaughn was offered an opportunity to become the chief arranger at Dot Records, a chance he readily accepted. He moved to Gallatin, Tennessee, where, in the course of time, his clients included not only the Hilltoppers but also Pat Boone, the Fontane Sisters, Gale Storm, and Eddy Arnold. (Eddy Arnold was contracted to RCA Victor, but Vaughn did arrangements for companies other than Dot.) When Dot ultimately moved to California, Billy went with the company. He also started his own orchestra, which became internationally famous, especially for such songs as "A Swinging Safari," "The Shifting, Whispering Sands," and, his biggest hit, "Melody of Love," a remake of an old Wayne King song.

Billy's replacement in the Hilltoppers was Eddie Crowe, a young man from Jimmy's hometown of Lockport, New York. Eddie was into sports, having lettered in four in high school, and he also played trumpet and piano. After three years in the U.S. Air Force, Crowe studied at the University of Buffalo while playing piano at various Buffalo nightspots, before joining the Hilltoppers. Quite importantly for the Hilltoppers' performances he did brilliant impersonations of James Cagney, James Stewart, Robert Mitchum, and several others. The Hilltoppers' performances were in no danger of lagging, but Crowe's impersonations added to audience enjoyment.[41]

In just eleven months, from April 1952 to March 1953,

when Jimmy Sacca was drafted into the army, the Hilltoppers had ascended from a group that was almost unknown even on the local level to a nationally acknowledged performing group, popular especially on the jukeboxes of America. The school newspaper, the *College Heights Herald,* rhapsodized that the Hilltoppers' rise to the top in so short a time "is indication . . . that one doesn't have to be from any of the larger cities to hit the top in the entertainment field." One can only speculate what would have happened if the original group of Vaughn, Sacca, McGuire, and Spiegelman had stayed together for a dozen or so years. They could very well have reached greater heights than they did. They were, however, as subject to time and tide as anyone, and so they coped with losses, additions, and national emergencies. They had stormy days ahead of them, and they dealt with them as well as they could.[42]

3 "Mixed-up" Hilltoppers

One of the songs the Hilltoppers put "in the can" (that is, recorded to be released periodically) was a snappy little love song, "From the Vine Came the Grape." It dealt with a lover being back with his girlfriend on the island of Capri. To the delight of listeners everywhere, Jimmy Sacca sang much of this song in Italian, adding an operatic touch to the performance.

Several months after the recording was released, Jimmy told a disc jockey that "he was not good at the lyrics" in "From the Vine." That was, he said, because the Hilltoppers only had one night at Dot recording studios in Gallatin, and he had not memorized the words. He had to sing them as they were held in front of him. Judging from the great success the song enjoyed, it didn't matter whether Jimmy had to read the words. (Another group, the Gaylords, also recorded "From the Vine," and their version outsold the Hilltoppers', to their chagrin—at least during the first year after its release.)

The Hilltoppers got a big boost when their publicity agent in Chicago, Dave Knorn, sent a small packet of grapes to every disc jockey in the area, with a message: "From the Vine Came the Grape; the squeezins' will come later." After a week or so, Knorn visited local DJs, accompanied by a beautiful model wearing only a bathing suit, despite the Chicago winter, and presented the "squeezin's'" to them. They came in the form of a miniature bottle of Mogen David wine, labeled "The wine from the Grapes which came from the Vine—The Hilltoppers."[1]

In addition to recording successes, three of the original Hilltoppers—Seymour Spiegelman, Don McGuire, and Jimmy Sacca—still had classroom responsibilities. Their schedule annoyed some professors and amused others. The three went to class only four days a week, almost always missing Fridays. Jimmy, Don, and Seymour had to pick and choose professors they thought would be the most lenient toward their absences, failure to do homework, and nodding off in class. Only now and then did they succeed.

Their personal pilot, Wilbur Parrish, flew them to one city after another. In some instances, they would give a dozen performances over a span of two and a half days. Because they limited their engagements to weekends, they were able to accept only $20,000 out of the first $150,000 offered to them.[2]

A part of their busy schedule in late 1952 and early 1953 included local as well as national performances. For example, they sang for chapel in Van Meter Auditorium—undoubtedly conjuring up some memories, fond and otherwise—when Vice President Alben Barkley came to town. The quartet entertained basketball fans at halftime in Murfreesboro, Tennessee, when Western and Middle Tennessee clashed, as well as at a home game with the University of Cincinnati. They also performed for Lions Club meetings in Bowling Green, as well as for a Mothers' Club gathering in Taylorsville, Kentucky.

On the national scene, they were guests on the Perry Como, Patti Page, Sammy Kaye, and Kate Smith shows, and they sang "From the Vine Came the Grape" for Dave Garroway on the

Today Show. Other appearances included *American Bandstand,* the Morrison Theater in Chicago, and a Cleveland charity show to raise money for community nursing programs. They played in nightclubs, theaters, and ballrooms in Toledo, Youngstown, Akron, and Lorain, Ohio; Brooklyn; Pittsburgh; Englewood Cliffs, New Jersey; Manhattan, and Philadelphia; they made several appearances at the Casa Loma in St. Louis, Missouri. The three students would generally be back in the classroom the following Monday morning. It was a grueling life, but one they greatly savored.[3]

Many fans remarked that each of the Hilltoppers had a "distinctive" voice. As they sang, one could clearly distinguish Don, Sy, and Billy from one another, and certainly Sacca from the other three. Though they were harmonious, they were also individualistic. They were voted by *Cashbox* magazine "the top vocal group of 1953." As columnist Joe Creason had said before, their classmates at the beginning of each week had no idea of what Jimmy, Don, and Seymour had done over the weekend—or why they were sometimes pretty sleepy.[4]

In late February 1953, just before he was to be graduated from Western, Jimmy Sacca got his "greetings" from Uncle Sam. That he was to report for duty March 13 did not reassure superstitious Hilltopper fans, because this date in 1953 fell on a Friday.[5]

The day before Jimmy had to leave, his hometown of Lockport wined and dined him. Headed by Lockport mayor William A. Matllet, some three hundred citizens gathered at the Hotel Lox Plaza for a combination dinner-variety show. Jackie Diehl's band performed during and after the festivities, with Allen Few as master of ceremonies. "Streamers, posters, circulars and other displays" were put up all over the city "to honor Jim for his homecoming." Of course, no program honoring Jimmy Sacca would be complete without his own performance. To the delight of his hometown neighbors and fan club members, he sang "Trying."[6]

Jimmy reported most immediately to Fort Devins, in Massachusetts. He was soon transferred to Fort Dix, New Jersey, and quickly assigned to a special services unit. This meant that at least two weekends a month he could leave base and perform with the Hilltoppers, particularly if they were playing on the eastern seaboard. In September 1953 he received his first leave, and for a brief period the Hilltoppers were almost back up to full steam again.[7]

On one of Jimmy's weekend passes, the Hilltoppers got together in St. Louis as the guests of Ed Bonner on radio station KXOK, where about two hundred children from all over the city came to hear them talk and sing. The children were not the only visitors. Seymour's fiancée, Jeannie Warren (who was also a student at Western), came to the studio. Jeannie was born in St. Louis but had lived most of her life in Moulton, a little town in north Alabama.

Bonner asked Seymour, "Who is the young lady in the audience?" Sy sheepishly replied, "Oh, that's my fiancée."

Bonner asked, "Are you going to get married?"

"Oh, no. Uh-uh," was the response. Seymour explained that their plans were for June 1954.

Later in the Bonner program, Don wanted to say hello to three of his friends in Missouri. Bonner noted that they were all girls. Don nonchalantly replied, "Oh, that's not all my girlfriends. I have others." He went on to read a commercial for

Leonards of St. Louis, a formal-suiting business. Bonner remarked that "he [McGuire] whistles when he mis-pronounces words, which is rather often. . . . Don has a very deep bass voice, a Kentucky drawl, and none too good English—typical of Kentuckians."[8]

They performed at St. Louis's Casa Loma Ballroom for three nights and one matinee. They also appeared at the Kresge five-and-ten-cent store in downtown St. Louis, where they gave away pictures, buttons, and other Hilltopper paraphernalia. St. Louis practically adopted the Hilltoppers, almost becoming, like Bowling Green and Gallatin, a home base.

Jimmy's departure for the army prompted a major reorganization of the Hilltoppers. Recent graduate Don McGuire was practice-teaching at Western's training school and Seymour Spiegelman had begun graduate work at the George Peabody College in Nashville. Moreover, military service for Don and Sy was, as it had been for Jimmy, an almost sure occurrence in the near future. The Hilltoppers would soon see a number of new faces. Hilltopper fans steadfastly argued that all these "mixtures" were temporary, and that the original group would ultimately reunite. From early 1953 to mid-1956 Jimmy Sacca (even though he spent much of that time in the army) was the most constant member of the original Hilltoppers. Other singers, including Eddie Crowe, Clive Dill, Bob Gaye, Lou Mastor, Karl Garvin, and, in the late fifties, Doug Cardoza filled in from time to time for missing Hilltoppers. Dill and Gaye came on board to replace Don and Sy when they were inducted into the U.S. Army in 1955.

Clive Dill majored in drama and music at Yale University and was a featured vocalist with the glee club, once having the honor to sing solos before the king and queen of the Netherlands. After Yale, Dill performed in a Broadway musical, *Bless You All,* and then became a singer for the Fred Waring choral group. His youthful ambition had been to be a foreign correspondent, but "the success of The Hilltoppers . . . changed this ambition to another—to be a featured singer in [his] own right." Through his acquaintance with Crowe and Sacca, Dill became a Hilltopper.[9]

Bob Gaye was a "diversified and accomplished" musician, and a "brilliant vocalist." He studied singing at the Brooklyn Conservatory of Music. He was a bass player, adding one more instrument to the Hilltopper ensemble. He had performed in the past with Johnny Ray and Sammy Davis Jr.[10]

The Hilltoppers got together "to warble like they used to back at Western State College," reported Bill Ladd's Almanac, in the *Louisville Courier-Journal.* The group did a lot of singing during the Christmas season, "but probably, didn't sing, 'I'll Be Home For Christmas,'" Ladd noted. They were doing seven shows a day at the Chicago Theatre. (Jimmy took leave from Fort Dix for these shows.)[11]

The arrangement for Jimmy to join his colleagues two or three times a month came to an abrupt halt in mid-1954, when he was transferred to Fort Buckner, in Okinawa. His absence stopped Hilltopper personal appearances, though the group did remain popular on jukeboxes and with the recording industry. Again, in anticipation of Jimmy's departure for foreign parts, the group had recorded several songs for systematic release in the months ahead.

While in Okinawa, PFC Jimmy Sacca formed another musical group, the Four Gunners, who wore striped coats and straw hats and sang in the manner of a barbershop quartet. In August 1954 the group, which, besides Jimmy, included Stanton Krock, Jefferson Osbourn, and Alfred B. Holt, entered an all-Okinawa singing contest, pitting their skills against several other military quartets. To a packed house, they sang "The Old Song" and "After Dark," taking first place. At the end of the competition, all groups joined together to sing such old favorites as "Little Brown Jug," "Heart of My Hearts," and "Let Me Call You Sweetheart," all to the delight of their fellow soldiers.[12]

The winning quartet got a trip to Tokyo, plus $40 each in cash, to compete in the U.S. Armed Forces Far East Barbershop Quartet Contest. The Four Gunners did not win, but Sacca got his first, important, taste of Japan. This country figured in his and the Hilltoppers' future careers.[13]

The military draft decimated the original Hilltopper group. Jimmy Sacca was discharged in March 1955, right when Seymour Spiegelman and Don McGuire were beginning their military service. Seymour, like Jimmy before him, was stationed at Fort Dix, and he, too, became part of a Special Services unit. He sang in the post's military chorus, which frequently performed on New York's WABC-Television, on a show hosted by Arlene Francis. Both Don and Sy stayed stateside during their military stints, but they were so widely separated that it was not feasible to attempt appearances by the original group.[14]

Military duty led to the hiring of additional replacements to perform with Jimmy while the tenor and the bass were away. The replacements had a great deal of talent, but the mixed group just wasn't the same for the large group of die-hard Hilltopper fans. But, as one of their admirers said, "At considerable financial sacrifice and with no fanfare Jimmy Sacca [along with

Sy Spiegelman and Don McGuire] did [their] duty." They certainly did not try to get any exemptions or deferments because of their status in the entertainment world. They served their country willingly and honorably.[15]

Karl Garvin, a new replacement, was originally from California but made his home in Tennessee. One of his associates in the Nashville Symphony was Western Kentucky music professor Bennie Beach. Just as Eddie Crowe had used his skills of mimicry as a Hilltopper innovation, Garvin, who succeeded Gaye as a Hilltopper, provided some instrumentation other than the piano that the Hilltoppers had always used. He was an accomplished trumpet player; and included in his repertory, was "Oh Mein Papa!" as popularized by Eddie Fisher and trumpet player Eddie Calvert.

Lou Mastor, another replacement, ultimately joined Garvin, as the two of them substituted for Dill and Gaye, when the latter went elsewhere. Mastor later went on a few tours with the revitalized Hilltoppers and joined in singing "The Kentuckian" for the movie of the same name, starring Burt Lancaster. One fan said in 1955 that "Jimmy never sounded better" but feared that jukebox patrons and records buyers would lose interest in the Hilltoppers because "they are so mixed up right now."[16]

On March 5, 1953, just a scant eight days before Jimmy left for military duty, the Hilltoppers appeared on *The Art Ford Show* on WNEW, New York, to receive a gold record for "P.S. I Love You." It was a poignant occasion: the Hilltoppers realized how far they had come in such a short time and wondered where they were going in the future.

Despite the "mix-ups," on January 12, 1954, eight months

before Jimmy shipped out to Okinawa, the Hilltoppers appeared on *The Milton Berle Show.* The show opened with the Hilltoppers standing around in plain clothes; the W sweaters and the beanies were gone, at least on this occasion. (Don McGuire did not perform on the Berle show because he was back at Western, taking a required exam.) Milton Berle whizzed by, pretending at first not even to see them, saying to his audience that he was "in a hurry." Then he returned to the screen, talking about a "stolen song." This led into the Hilltoppers' rendition of their best-known song at the time, "P.S. I Love You."[17]

Jimmy got an extra slot on the show to sing a brand-new song entitled "You're All That I Need." The author of this song was Milton Berle himself. Berle asked Jimmy, "Who wrote the song?" Jimmy replied, "You did, Mr. Berle." Berle then asked, "Who wrote the lyrics?" and Jimmy answered, "You did." Berle asked, "How many records do you think it will sell?" And Jimmy responded, "How many relatives have you got?" Jimmy sang the song solo, and tenderly, winning much acclaim from the audience.[18]

Though their personal appearances were less frequent while Jimmy served in the army, the Hilltoppers maintained a great popularity on the jukeboxes of America and with the recording industry. In March 1954, for example, "Poor Butterfly" (in which Jimmy put to very good use his vowel implosions, or echo chamber) was released. Within days it was number ten in sales in St. Louis and number three in Pittsburgh and was "going strong" in Duluth, Minnesota, and other parts of the Upper Midwest. Soon it was on the honor roll of hits in music stores throughout the United States. Another 1954 release was "Till Then" (also recorded by the Mills Brothers). It was tremendously popular throughout the United States and most of Western Europe, especially in England.

Doug Cardoza was another replacement for an absent Hilltopper. Cardoza was a student at Western and a relative of Spiegelman's, so he was more readily accepted as a part of the group than the others. Hilltopper fans continued to believe that these interruptions were only temporary and that soon the original Hilltoppers with the oversized sweaters emblazoned with Ws, the white buck shoes, the beanie caps, and the collegiate spirit would soon be back. Only partially did these fans realize their dreams.

Everywhere the Hilltoppers performed, a fan club was almost immediately organized. After just a short time, there were over four hundred of these clubs scattered throughout the country, each made up of forty to fifty people, all dedicated to Hilltopper fortunes. One of the earliest and most active clubs was in Chicago; headed by Judy Ehlert, the group called themselves "the Hilltopperettes." In their exuberance, the members of this club set the standard for fan clubs everywhere: they were anything but passive. On the contrary, sometimes they were quite pushy in getting attention for their heroes.

The rapid rise of these fan clubs, and their enthusiasm, countered the thinking of a wide range of intellectuals that "mass culture" was somehow wrong for the "masses." The loudest critics of mass culture (to which, of course, the Hilltoppers belonged), were "neo-Marxist highbrows who feared the loss of . . . high culture and stressed that mass culture was becoming a narcotic that left the working class docile, incapable of recognizing its own oppression." Among the earliest critics of the "culture industry" were members of the so-called Frankfurt school, a group of researchers associated with the Marxist Institut für Sozialforschung (Institute for Social Research). Frankfurt school member Theodor Adorno held that mass culture led to mass passivity, rendering citizens observers of life rather than participants in it. Adorno therefore argued that mass culture was "pernicious" and more likely to "serve totalitarian rather than democratic ends," being tainted with both "bourgeois ideology and industrialism."[19]

Mass culture also had its defenders, starting around the early 1960s. At first, they promoted middle-class culture against the highbrows, and argued that mass culture techniques were not pernicious as long as they were not excessive. They argued that mass culture did not amount to a governmental offering of *panem et circenses* (bread and circuses) to the citizens to cause widespread lack of interest in how they were ruled. Music of all kinds was caught up in the "cultural wars" of the sixties and seventies. The members of fan clubs of groups like the Hilltoppers were generally well read; in no way did they reflect the fawning, docile images feared by the Frankfurt school and its adherents.

The main job of a fan club, of course, is to promote the good fortunes and well-being of the performer or performers it supports. The Hilltopperettes offered membership to anyone interested for $10 a year and offered memorabilia for sale. The early fan club members envisioned a time when they could sell Hilltopper identification bracelets as well as lapel buttons. They began to sell snapshots of the Hilltoppers for a dime each, and they planned to wear specific uniforms whenever they attended Hilltoppers concerts. For winter they wanted gray or green slacks, red sweaters with huge Hs emblazoned on them, white collars, and red-and-white beanies. For summer, the uniform would be red pedal pushers or skirts, white shirts with small Hs, and red-and-white beanies. Members would also receive a wallet-sized photo of the Hilltoppers and the address of a like-minded pen pal if they wanted one.[20]

As it turned out, the biggest fan of them all was a teenager from Mayfield, Kentucky, Bobbie Ann Mason, who would later go on to fame as a novelist, short story writer, and essayist. On February 22, 1953, she wrote a letter to Western president Paul Garrett wanting to know what sports each Hilltopper liked, which of the four had been graduated, and what Don McGuire was teaching at the university's Training School. "As you are the President of the College and know most of your students by name, I thought you might be able to give me this information." Director of public affairs Robert Cochran answered Mason's letter on March 4, telling her that McGuire was teaching physical education and that Sacca would probably come back to Western "unless his success in the music world will make it impossible from a financial standpoint to stop singing."[21]

Mason formed what ultimately became the largest Hilltopper fan club in the country and, after the Chicago model, called it "the Hill-topper-ettes." In late spring 1954 she wrote once again to Western, this time to the college alumni/ae office. "As you know, one of the most wonderful things ever to happen to Western is the singing Hilltoppers. They couldn't come from a better school," she wrote. She said she was "very glad" the Hilltoppers "attended the best college in Kentucky." (A few years later, she matriculated at the University of Kentucky, in Lexington.) She also inquired about procuring a copy of the *Tal-*

isman, Western's yearbook. Again, Robert Cochran answered her: "The singing Hilltoppers have gone far," he said, "and will go much further in the music world. All four of the boys are extremely nice young men and deserve every bit of the success that may come their way." And a *Talisman,* he mentioned to her, would set her back $6. She never bought one.[22]

She wrote also to presidential assistant Kelly Thompson, who forwarded her letter to Don McGuire, telling him, on May 28, 1954, "to give this little girl [Mason] all the information you can as she is one of your most ardent admirers." Of course, McGuire wrote back (or at least the secretary at Dot Records, Maxine Caruthers, did), starting a friendship that lasts even today. Don gave her much information about Billy, Jimmy, and Sy—their favorite sports, favorite foods, and so on—which she began to incorporate into the Hilltoppers fanzine.[23]

What inspired Bobbie Ann Mason to become one of the first presidents of the Hilltopper fan clubs, first locally and then nationally? Like most teenagers, Mason loved music of all sorts. Tony Martin, Perry Como, Patti Page—she couldn't get enough of them. On Saturday nights, she would tune in to WLAC in Nashville to hear a DJ called John R., who played "raunchy, stomping-and-shouting blues numbers by black singers like Big Bill Broonzy and Memphis Slim and Little Junior Parker, Little Walter, T-Bone Walker, Elmore James and Big Joe Turner."[24]

Gene Nobles, another Nashville DJ, played "droopy-drawers songs" (the slow stuff) and "mean, low-down songs." He played many releases from Dot Records. Mason liked all of the label's performers, including Pat Boone (whom the fan club newsletter later made an "Honorary Hilltopper," an appointment he thoroughly savored) and the Fontane Sisters. But her favorite group was the Hilltoppers.[25]

"The Hilltoppers, I decided, represented everything I had ever felt and dreamed about my life." Their style, Mason said, "wasn't exactly Big Bill Broonzy and it wasn't rock and roll yet either . . . but it grabbed me and shook me up like a religious vision, a calling." (Did what many southerners regarded as Jimmy's implosive "revivalist" singing have anything to do with this "calling"?) She continued: "My passion for music transmuted to simon-pure hero worship. . . . A Kentucky singing quartet had achieved national fame!" She even began to recommend Norman Vincent Peale's book *The Power of Positive Thinking* as a way to get people to pay attention to the singing Hilltoppers.[26]

The most important job of the fan clubs was to contact all the disc jockeys, not only in the immediate area, but also around the region and country. Mason and her cohorts meticulously wrote down the names of all the DJs they thought might play newly released Hilltopper songs. These included Joe Bleaux, Blytheville, Arkansas; Roy Raymer, Chicago; Fred Wolfe, Detroit; Ed Bonner, St. Louis (who turned out to be particularly well-disposed toward the Hilltoppers—St. Louis "almost became their second home"); Dick Clark, Philadelphia; Anny Starr and Jerry Marshall, New York City; and scores of others. As part of a national program to publicize the Hilltoppers, Mason recommended that each member of the fan club write one request each to ten different disc jockeys around the country. This would amount to hundreds of requests for DJs to play the recordings of the most popular jukebox group in the country at the time. Most of them did, to the great advantage of the singing group.

In 1955 the Kentucky Hilltopper fan club came out with a new fanzine, *Hilltopper Topics.* Mason did most of the writing, but she encouraged everyone to write for the paper. She printed anything and everything she thought would benefit "the guys." One way of promoting Hilltopper songs was to write loving parodies of them. Thus, to the tune of " D-A-R-L-I-N," Maurine Balluff wrote "Hilltoppers":

H means they're like heaven, like the clouds that float above.
I means they're the idols that I love.
L and L for light that they give me each new day.
T is that they're tops in every way.
O is for the obstacles that always seem to be
P and P for praying God will see;
E and R—endurance, with the S the stars they are now
That is all the words that 'Darlin' will allow! [27]

And, of course, in the wonderful exuberance of youth, Hilltopper cheers were not too far behind:

Billy Billy he's our man; if he can't do it, Seymour can.
Seymour, Seymour, he's our man; if he can't do it, Don can.
Don, Don he's our man, if he can't do it, Jimmy can.
Jimmy, Jimmy, he's our man; if he can't do it, NOBODY CAN!

And another one: "1, 2, 3, 4, 5, 6, 7, All good fan clubs go to Heaven. When they get there, they will say 'Hilltoppers! Hilltoppers! They're O.K.'" And yet another one: "2 bits, 4 bits, 6 bits a dollar. All for the Hilltoppers, stand up and holler. Yea!!!" [28]

The national Hilltopper fan club brought together about three hundred affiliated groups that had been formed all over the country. As might be expected, there was an avid Hilltopper fan club in Lockport, New York, Jimmy's hometown, headed by Pat Pusateri. Each year this fan club sponsored, in cooperation with the local Kiwanis, a Teen-Age Day to honor young people. In 1955, the Lockport group was able to have as the celebration's chief guests the Hilltoppers themselves. A club functioned in Seneca Falls, New York, where Seymour hailed from. Other active clubs included Pittsburgh, headed by Arlene Weithershausen; Cambridge, Massachusetts, headed by Mary Hanley; and Verona, New Jersey, with Frances Brogan in charge.[29]

In Mount Vernon, Illinois, Carolyn Braddy tended to Hilltopper fortunes. She and a group of high school boys pantomimed a Hilltopper number, "Do the Bop," in a variety show at her school and actually did the bop during the performance. Dorothy Clark, from Sewell, New Jersey, and her local Hilltopper Club sponsored a dance, the proceeds of which went to the American Red Cross. And Betti Becker, Hilltopper president in Kansas City, Missouri, wrote an article on the Hilltoppers for *Prom Magazine.*

In Gallatin, Dot Records secretary Maxine Caruthers offered assistance in keeping these numerous Hilltopper fan clubs going. Many of the more than four hundred Hilltopper fan clubs became inactive over time, especially when all of the substitutions of the original singers began. With Jimmy's return in March 1955, however, things began to percolate once again. Jimmy asked Caruthers to work with Mason in appointing more national officers, helping to create new clubs and reactivate old ones.[30]

In the interest of national effectiveness, there were thoughts about making Bobbie Ann Mason and Judy Ehlert copresidents, each presiding in her own area. "I wish that you and Judy would get together about the national office," Jimmy wrote to Mason, "and decide about an office that will take in all the clubs, including the Hilltopperettes, for I feel a need for one national office." For a time, apparently, it was decided that Bobbie and Judy would be copresidents. But Caruthers wrote Mason claiming that Jimmy did not want Bobbie and Judy to be listed as "co-presidents of the national organization," because "some other leaders [of local groups] might get their feelings hurt." Thus, Mason remained the only national Hilltopper fan club president. She and her mother and her friend Carolyn Braddy sometimes traveled to Hilltopper performances, where they were frequently recognized by Jimmy or someone else on stage, publicly thanking Bobbie for her assistance. Sometimes, the Hilltoppers took their special guests home in their big blue Fleetwood Cadillac.[31]

No amount of fan club activity, however, could stem the tide against which the Hilltoppers seemed to be swimming in the mid-fifties. For one thing, their base of operations, Dot Records, moved from Gallatin to Hollywood. And going with Randy Wood was Billy Vaughn. Although Billy had not performed with the Hilltoppers for some time, he still arranged many of their songs. Now he was going to be more than two thousand miles from them. Although the Hilltoppers were now booked by MCA Entertainment, they needed Billy, not only for his musical abilities, but also for his constant encouragement. Despite Randy's and Billy's assurances to the contrary, it seemed clear that this move to California boded ill for Hilltopper publicity.

Moreover, the Hilltoppers were, as always, most popular in the eastern part of the country. They had not caught on in San Francisco as well as they had in New York. Some argued that Dot Records' move to California would help the Hilltoppers with publicity in the West. Even before the move, a few Dot Records officials were making plans to launch Hilltoppers promotional programs among West Coast disc jockeys. Others maintained, however, that geographical distances would put the group and the company at a mutual disadvantage, and thus lead to neglect. There is no evidence to support the latter assertion; nevertheless, it is undeniable that the distance between Gallatin, Tennessee, and Hollywood, California, is great. Wood sold Dot Records to Paramount Pictures in 1957 for $3 million, severing yet another direct tie between the Hilltoppers and Dot Records.[32]

Another disconcerting factor for the Hilltoppers was that rock 'n' roll seemed to have appeared overnight (almost in the same way the Hilltoppers had). Elvis Presley, Buddy Holly, Pat Boone, Ricky Nelson, and Fats Domino, to say nothing of Bill Haley and the Comets and others, were quickly changing the landscape of popular music all over the world. When the Hilltoppers recorded their first record, "Trying," it was 1952, well before the rock 'n' roll era. By early 1957, when the original group was mostly back together, they attempted some rock 'n' roll themselves ("Do the Bop," for example), but by this time they were too far behind current musical fashions. The U.S. military draft and the changing moods and fancies of the listening public changed the Hilltoppers' fortunes, unfortunately, forever. Music is always evolving, and if a group does not keep up, it will become outdated.[33]

After Jimmy's return from the military, the group was made up of Jimmy Sacca, Eddie Crowe, Clive Dill, and Bob Gaye. Though their public appearances were somewhat curtailed—some DJs were now asking, "Who are the Hilltoppers?"— the changes in the group's composition were beginning to cause some confusion. There were even rumors that the original Hilltoppers would never reunite. Jimmy scotched these thoughts as he wrote to Mason that Crowe, Dill, and Gaye "are just temporary, and they know it. There won't be any confusion when Don and Seymour are with us again. We realize that the public won't ever take to this group as they have to the original Hilltoppers, and we can assure you [of] our re-uniting again."[34]

From March 1955, when Jimmy was discharged, to the end of the year, the Hilltoppers spent a great deal of time reestablishing themselves, especially in personal appearances. In September 1955, they had two performances in St. Louis, both for KXOK, as guests of their old friend Ed Bonner, who had always been an ardent fan. On the air on September 23, Bonner and his colleague, Bruce Hayward, welcomed Jimmy home from military service and asked for a brief history of the Hilltoppers. Jimmy spoke so much about Dot Records that Bonner reminded him that the program was sponsored by the Mendenhall Ford Dealers of St. Louis. The next day the group was back on KXOK for additional songs, conversations, and call-ins from fans. To the pleasure of everyone, the group sang the theme song from the movie *The Kentuckian,* as well as "Searching."[35]

The next month, the Hilltoppers were in Chicago, performing—along with Liberace—at the Chicago Theatre. Their host was Steve Schickels, a DJ at radio station WGN, who hosted a program called *Inside Show Business.* At the Chicago Theatre Liberace's piano took up much of the front of the stage. Under these circumstances, the Hilltoppers would not be able to see the audience very well. They had always interacted well with audiences, frequently going right to the edge of the stage to shake hands and receive bouquets and other compliments. Fortunately, Liberace dismantled all of his personal effects at the end of his performances and left the Hilltoppers to their audiences.[36]

One of the Hilltoppers' biggest hits in 1955 was "Only You" (recorded as well by the Ink Spots and the Platters). Caruthers wrote to Mason: "'Only You,' is going strong. I surely hope it will be a hit for the boys because they surely deserve one after waiting and trying so long." Then she divulged to Mason some information of which most fans were unaware. "Only You" was sung by Jimmy Sacca, but he was not accompanied by the rest of the Hilltoppers. Instead, a couple of singers from the NBC chorus in Chicago performed in the background. Increasingly, it became the practice for Dot Records to send Jimmy, as lead singer, to various recording sites and have studio singers join him. Thus, when fans listened to the Hilltoppers on the jukebox or a record, the only known singer involved was Jimmy Sacca.[37]

The Hilltoppers' early 1956 recording of "Do the Bop," which never made the charts, was said by many to be an effort to fulfill the "floods of requests" for the group to perform some rock 'n' roll. Billy Vaughn wrote the song, adding a touch of the original group to the record. The flip side to "Do the Bop" was "When You're Alone." Another recording soon followed with "Faded Rose" and "So Tired."[38]

On their way to Evansville, Indiana, their car (still a Fleetwood Cadillac) had a flat tire, and their spare had no air in it. With the help of some local citizens, they were soon on their way again. Their other performances from March to May 1956, included Ames, Marion, Clear Lake, and Sioux Falls, Iowa; Grand Rapids, Michigan; Oak Lawn, Illinois; and Canton and Cincinnati, Ohio. By this time, the Hilltoppers had once again been reorganized. Crowe and Gaye were out, and Mastor and Garvin were in. In the case of Garvin, it was back in, for he had substituted for Don McGuire in the past when Don was unable to get away from school.

In January 1956, the group was in New Orleans, performing at Liller's Nightclub, before moving on to the Shamrock Hotel in Houston. One afternoon, during a break in their performances, Jimmy decided to go to the racetrack. "The P.A. system called my name," he recalled, and he had a message to report to the downtown police station. Bob Gaye (whose real name, as it turned out, was Robert Goldstein) had been arrested on a narcotics charge. Authorities found "a tobacco can containing marijuana shreddings enough to make twenty cigarettes."[39]

Gaye readily admitted to the use of marijuana. "Trying to please the public at night is a hard job. Man, I've got to relax when I finish work. . . . I believe that smoking marijuana as long as it doesn't lead to something else, is not as bad as drinking." He was not an addict, he said, and "I never sold it or encouraged anyone else to use it."[40]

Sacca dismissed him on the spot. "If we'd known he was on junk, we'd have fired him [immediately]," Sacca said. Then he made a telephone call to New York, where he found Karl Garvin to join the group for its forthcoming appearances in Texas. Garvin stayed with the group for the next several months.[41]

News spread quickly throughout New Orleans about the Hilltoppers' troubles. On their last night at Liller's, they sang as a trio. If Sacca, Crowe, and Dill had had any misgivings about audience reaction to a narcotics charge and to a trio instead of a quartet, they quickly learned that they had nothing to fear. "It was their biggest night since we opened," said a jubilant club owner, J. Liller. "The crowd was with them all the way." After enthusiastic applause and several encores, the Hilltoppers knew they were as popular as they had ever been.

A few weeks after the Gaye narcotics incident, Sacca met up with Bobbie Ann Mason in Vincennes, Indiana. "Well, what did you think when you heard the news?" was one of his first questions. He was, of course, referring to the police business and its attendant unwanted publicity in New Orleans. "I was shocked," Bobbie Ann replied, although she claimed that she had never heard of marijuana. Jimmy told her that he had had no idea Gaye was "using the stuff. I fired him so fast he didn't know what hit him." Bobbie Ann, loyal Hilltopper fan that she was, told Jimmy that Gaye was not "one of the real Hilltoppers. I longed for the day when Sy and Don would rejoin the group." Alas, it would be at least another year before this happy event occurred.[42]

Although the start of 1956 was not auspicious for the Hilltoppers, it was nevertheless to be a year of defining moments. The draft continued to take its toll, as did the increasing popularity of rock 'n' roll. Dot Records' move to California was not particularly reassuring to the Hilltoppers because, among other things, it left them wondering where "home" was. For the past several months, it had been Gallatin, under the watchful eye of Randy Wood, owner and CEO of Dot Records.

Moreover, by the mid-fifties, all of the original Hilltoppers had married and started a family. Billy was married to Marion "Smitty" Smith, even at the time the group was formed, and the couple had two sons, Rick and Al, and a daughter, Zona.

Jimmy Sacca met a young lady from Mississippi, Annie Rivers Holloway, who was attending the Bowling Green Business University. The two were obviously smitten with each other, and their marriage produced three sons, James III, Terry, and Thomas. While Jimmy was in the service, Annie sometimes lived with him on base, but for the most part they made their home in Mississippi.

Seymour married his fiancée, Jeannie Warren. After their wedding, Sy spent most of his time in Alabama. Their family ultimately consisted of two daughters, Suellyn and Penelope, and a son, Brett. Seymour's daughter, Kimberly, was born during Seymour's second marriage, to Pauline Russo.

Don married Maxine McIntosh, from Owensboro, Kentucky, where they made their home for several years. Their children were Don Kreis, Lisa, and Cindy.

Then, in mid-1956, an event occurred that rejuvenated the Hilltoppers; their present make up now consisted of Jimmy Sacca, Eddie Crowe, Lou Mastor, and Karl Garvin. They were thrilled to have been invited to make an extended tour of several weeks in the British Isles, starting in July. It was the first of the overseas trips the Hilltoppers were soon to be experiencing, and those excursions made musical history.

4 "Blimey, We've Gone Limey"

"You probably know that we're leaving for England, and we really are looking forward to this trip," the Hilltoppers wrote to the readers of that "wonderful journal," the national fanzine *Hilltopper Topics.* "Only You" had almost gone off the charts in mid-1956 in England, where a few newspapers described it as a "rock 'n' roll ballad." Surprisingly even though it was now four years old, "Trying" had not even been heard in England, or at least it had not been played regularly by disc jockeys. The Hilltoppers considered this their signature song and were willing to hold off its performance until they were actually there in person. Any tour of the British Isles that featured "Trying" could only bolster their reputation at this point.[1]

Jimmy Sacca, Eddie Crowe, Karl Garvin, and Lou Mastor arrived in the early morning of July 5, 1956, at London's Heathrow Airport. To the interest and amusement of their hosts, they were wearing beanies and sweaters with a big W in the middle, "referring . . . to ex-students" of Western Kentucky State College (which was not exactly true). One reporter mentioned their "massive red sweaters," with a "mysterious" W "slashed boldly upon them." (Did it ever occur to the reporter that all she had to do was ask what the W stood for?)[2]

The group was met by a representative from London Records, a branch of the Decca Company. In its write-up about the Hilltoppers' arrival, the *London News Chronicle* referred to the four young men as "singing eggheads." At first they did not know whether to be depressed, insulted, or complimented by this characterization. Later, someone told them that "egghead," in England at least, means "intelligent," so the young men from Western Kentucky were mollified.[3]

Instantly, they suffered a series of culture shocks. The first one came when they were being driven, through the rain, of course, from the airport to their hotel, *"on the wrong side of the road!"* Well, yes, they'd heard all about how the English drove their cars and trucks (lorries) on the left, but it was still quite disconcerting when they actually experienced it. They adapted to this "strange custom" rather quickly, and ceased to expect instant chaos every time their driver met an oncoming vehicle.[4]

Another hurdle for the Hilltoppers, newly arrived in the Old Country, was language. "We speak English, don't we?" they asked. "The English speak English, don't they? So why do we have so much trouble understanding each other?" The Hilltoppers had just come face to face with famous playwright George Bernard Shaw's dictum that "England and America are two countries separated by a common language." Since their tour was eight weeks long, they became "official limey speakers" before they headed back for the United States.[5]

Of course, British audiences had only heard the Hilltoppers on jukeboxes and records; few had ever seen them in person. "So, in facing their British fans," one reporter claimed, "the Hilltoppers are also out to prove something: that in person, they can live up to the great expectations created on records." A confident Jimmy Sacca responded to this statement: "It's a challenge that I think we can meet." As their tour went on, this statement turned out to be very true.[6]

July 6, the day after their arrival in England, the Hilltoppers (jet lag and all) appeared on British television's *On the Town,* and two nights later they were on *The Jack Jackson Show.* They were booked at theatres and nightclubs all the way from London to the outer reaches of Scotland.

Their first major performance was on Monday, July 9, at London's Finsbury Park Empire. The initial offering was "I Feel a Song Coming On," followed by "I've Got the World on a String," and then they performed their first announced song, "Till Then." It was not really until the group sang "Do the Bop" that they got audience attention. Nevertheless, English and continental audiences did not consider the Hilltoppers' music to be rock 'n' roll. The Hilltoppers were singers of love ballads, and to a considerable extent "Do the Bop" was out of character for them.

The Hilltoppers received a great deal of press coverage while they were touring the British Isles. In attendance at Finsbury Park was critic Doug Geddes. He came already doubtful about the Hilltoppers' ability to entertain him, despite his claim that he had "no preconceived notions." The biggest claim to fame these young men had in England, he asserted, was "Only You," which had already been recorded by other groups like the Platters. Sure enough, critic Geddes, letting his "no preconceived" notions get the better of him, left the theatre after the Hilltopper performance "very unimpressed by the group as an act." He did admit, however, that he was "getting old."[7]

Monday night performances in British theatres (as probably in theatres throughout the world) were, generally speaking, sparsely attended. After all, it was the first work day of the week and was spent by thousands of people just recovering from the weekend. It could very well have been, therefore, that the majority of the audience that night was made up of the aging population. Retirees didn't have to go to work the next morning.

As the Hilltopper program progressed at Finsbury, they sang "Raining Teardrops," "I Must Be Dreaming," and then their "latest issue" (at least in England), "Trying." Even though this was their "signature song," there was a "detached coldness" about their performance. Perhaps this perceived "coldness" was due at least in part to the singers' weaving in and out of the microphones, much as they had been taught by Jon Gregory way back when they appeared on the Ed Sullivan show. The stage at Finsbury, as Geddes noted, was larger than the hotel cabaret floors where the Hilltoppers were accustomed to performing and achieving great intimacy with their audiences. The difference in size of the stage could have accounted for the "detached" feeling that Geddes believed some of the audience felt. This thought, however, was not affirmed by the applause of those who had come to see and hear the Hilltoppers.[8]

Geddes also had a problem with Jimmy Sacca's voice. "I found them [the Hilltoppers] pleasant and likeable, but would prefer to hear the group sing more often as a group, rather than have indigestible amounts of single voices from leader, Jimmy Sacca, backed only by the 'woo-wah' of the other three boys." He lauded Karl Garvin's renditions of "Oh My Papa" and the impersonations offered by Eddie Crowe, particularly those of James Cagney "singing" "Tutti Frutti." After this act, Karl came back on stage with a rousing trumpet rendition of "St. Louis Blues," to the delight of those in attendance.[9]

Another primarily negative review snidely remarked that "The Hilltoppers must have ridden in on the popularity wave at a time when utter simplicity was a gimmick." Though "Jimmy Sacca gave out energetically" and his three partners "mooed, cooed, and hummed" and the Hilltoppers did not engage in the "grotesque calisthenics" of some other groups, their performances "taxed the harmonic senses not a whit." Naturally, he did not go on to explain what he meant by "harmonic senses." To have done so would have lost the "cleverness" aspect of so many British reviews.[10]

One reviewer claimed that the "corny humour" (failing to define or give examples of "corny humour") of opening night would be gone by Tuesday. Mostly, it—whatever it was—was gone; but the reviewer said that Sacca's constant references to British audiences as "wonderful, wonderful," should be discouraged. (Maybe the phrase sounded too much like Lawrence Welk.) "We don't believe that," said the reviewer, apparently referring to the critical side of British audiences, "and we embarrass easily."[11]

While Geddes in some of his reviews of newer singing groups, including the Hilltoppers, described himself as "perturbed" and "antiquated," younger reporters were perhaps the most qualified to pass musical judgment. For one thing, they were closer in age to the Hilltoppers than Geddes and many of his veteran colleagues.

Donald Black, for example, admired the Hilltoppers' "relaxed style," noting that they looked "like college kids," casually dressed in their trademark red sweaters, beanies, and white buckskin shoes. Audiences, Black advised, should not expect too many "fast-paced" performances from the Hilltoppers, because they had largely built their reputations on slow-moving love ballads.[12]

Sacca was quickly compared to Bill Kenney on some of the original songs of the Ink Spots. Again, fans and critics alike remarked on Jimmy's "echo chamber" and the very effective "doo-wahs" and "doo-wops" of the harmonizing boys behind him. As their performances continued, Eddie widened his repertoire of impersonations, adding Robert Mitchum, Liberace, Ed Sullivan, and famed country singer Eddy Arnold. This was "British variety" at its best, and Black and other critics predicted that the Hilltoppers "would improve with every performance." The accuracy of this remark was borne out when the Hilltoppers' tour, originally scheduled for eight weeks, was increased to ten. There was no question about Hilltopper popularity in the mother country.[13]

Accentuating this popularity was the formation of the Hilltopper Club of Great Britain, headquartered in Slough, Buckinghamshire. One of its most ardent members, Dorothy Matt, attended a Hilltopper performance at the Empire Theatre in Durham and wrote to the fanzine about her experience. "Those four swell guys can sure put zest and life into any song they sing," she exulted. "Their style of singing," she continued, "has that extra something that other groups lack." After the performance, Dorothy went backstage for handshakes and autographs. During the handshake sessions, a friend called out to Dorothy, "It would be better if they kissed you." She wrote disappointedly, "Sorry to say, the boys did not oblige."[14]

In addition to soliciting reports and letters from its members, this English fan club also declared certain other performers "honorary members." In this way, Pat Boone, Guy Mitchell, Julius LaRosa, Tommy Steele, Alma Cogan, Frankie Laine, Ronnie Hilton, Eve Boswell, and numerous other show business personalities lent their names to boost Hilltopper fortunes. The fan club's directors and members also kept up a steady stream of correspondence to the British Broadcasting Corporation, to Radio Luxemburg, and to the Armed Forces Network, urging all outlets to showcase Hilltopper songs. "Keep the pressure on" was the message. It worked, because the Hilltoppers' popularity soared throughout the British Isles.

"The only way we can get the Hilltopper recordings into the top ten is for all club members to do their part and buy each of their records as they are released over here." This exhortation from fanzine directors Diane Gilham and Joyce Hands was accompanied by an announcement that the Hilltopper Fan Club was soon to meet jointly with the group supporting Bill Haley and the Comets. This was certain to be an extravaganza in which the fortunes of both singing groups would shoot up precipitously.[15]

Shortly after the Hilltoppers arrived in England, an event occurred that kept the famous British tabloids busy for several days, increasing attendance at their performances. A young lady, Dorothy McCain, flew into London from Germany to see Hilltopper Eddie Crowe. "If my family knew I was in England," McCain told reporters, "they'd go crazy." She was, she said, from Texas and, somewhat dubiously, claimed that it was "against Texas protocol"— since Eddie had never met her family— "to fall in love without an introduction." She wore an engagement ring but refused to identify its source.[16]

Reportedly, she and Eddie were "madly in love" with each other and had met some months before at a Texas supper club. Their "fling" in England apparently did not last very long. She was said to come from a wealthy Texas family, and her presence provoked much curiosity, even among those who did not particularly care for musical variety shows. Eddie and his three colleagues prudently made no comments to the press about McCain. When the Hilltoppers left for the north of England and Scotland, she was not with them. After a few days of intense interest, even the tabloids stopped mentioning her, and one more Hilltopper moment passed into history.[17]

Then, to their consternation, the Hilltoppers learned that back in the States Dot Records had just released a new song called "Ka-Ding-Dong." The featured soloist was Chuck Schroeder, singing with a group called the G-Clefs, or temporarily, the Hilltoppers! Randy Wood had formed another singing group, also named the Hilltoppers (apparently, there was no patent or copyright to the title) to take advantage of the popularity of rhythm and blues sweeping the country at the time. The *real* Hilltoppers were upset that "Randy Wood had a quick recording session using none of the original Hilltoppers . . . [to record a song] which he thought was going to be a big hit, and then he used their name to get quick airtime." Back home, fanzine *Hilltopper Highlights* picked up this story and rhetorically asked, "Where's Jimmy?" Nevertheless, fan clubs around the country strongly supported this version of "Ka-Ding-Dong," believing it would promote Hilltopper popularity. Schroeder's recording with "the Hilltoppers" did not seriously affect relations between Wood and *the* Hilltoppers. Throughout their long relationship with him, they trusted Wood to treat them right, so much so, that they never even felt a need to check the account books at Dot Records.[18]

Another momentary diversion for the Hilltoppers came when Jimmy, speaking for the entire group, said "show business is no feather bed" and agreed to participate in a cross-Channel swim from England to France. Jimmy asserted that show business people from opera singers to popular crooners often say that their kind of life calls for the stamina of an athlete. As leader of the Hilltoppers, Jimmy saw no difficulties in a cross-Channel swim: "You've got to be fit to stay at the top." After all, he had been a star football player at Western Kentucky College and had continued to be physically fit ever since and, of course, to be keenly interested in athletics of all kinds. Definitely, it required a great deal of strength and stamina to stay on the road and perform as much as he and his colleagues did.[19]

The cross-Channel swim was the brainchild of Billy Butlin, famed all over England for his camping, recreational, and entertainment centers. Butlin's idea was for each swimmer of a relay team to swim for ten or fifteen minutes at a time, and then rest for thirty minutes on an accompanying boat, while a teammate took his turn. Each half hour a team member would start again for another ten or fifteen minutes of rigorous swimming. The first team to arrive in France, some twenty or so miles away, would be wined and dined throughout the British Isles. There was certainly enough of a competitive spirit in Jimmy and the other Hilltoppers to go for it. The singing group convinced the authorities that they were healthy enough and received permission to participate. It would certainly be a great piece of publicity for future performances if the Hilltoppers could claim to be the first singing group ever to swim the English Channel![20]

Just before they were to board the train for the south of England they received a telephone call from the States. Dot wanted to release a long-playing record of the Hilltoppers while they were in Great Britain (one wonders why Dot could not have done the same thing with "Ka-Ding-Dong"). Unfortunately, someone back in the States had lost two of the numbers from this LP, and the final product could not be put together until the missing pieces were restored. So, instead of going to Dover, the group traveled to London, where they had to rerecord "I Can't Give You Anything but Love" and "Moonlight Becomes You." They had been in Edinburgh when the telephone call came. Their trip to London and then back to Scotland, said *TV Mirror,* must have been the "longest route ever from Edinburgh to Glasgow." Of course, the group was happy to do the rerecordings, but the singers were sorely disappointed that they were not able to demonstrate their athletic prowess—at least on this occasion.[21]

Since Jimmy had been a football player back in Kentucky, it was natural for him to attend some English football (or soccer, in American parlance) games. He made the acquaintance of Colin Grainger, well known "left winger" for England's international team, and, in fact, ran around the track at Bramall Lane with him on several occasions. After one of these exercises, Jimmy said to Colin, "Come along and see us [in concert]," and then, perhaps absent-mindedly, he added, "Better yet, come on stage and try your voice out."[22]

The famed football player accepted the invitation, and became an "un-billed item" at a Hilltopper concert at Sheffield's

Empire Theatre. One reporter quipped, "I trust there will be no strife between the Variety Artists Federation and the Football Players' Union" because of Grainger's "crooning" with Sacca and the Hilltoppers. In fact, Grainger sang "Walk Hand in Hand," and even joined Eddie Crowe in some much-appreciated impersonations.[23]

Not only was there no "strife" between federation and union; there was much acclamation. Grainger's appearance, accompanied by loud trumpet fanfares, was played up as "ballyhoo," as well it might have been, because it definitely got the public's attention. There was no "jiving in the aisles" but the audience did "sway in their seats" and "beat time with their hands and feet." The Hilltoppers, said one newspaper, were "supercharged" and at the same time "sugar sweet in sentiment. The audience couldn't get enough."[24]

Heady stuff, all this, for a group that was only four years old. It was a long way from Western's Van Meter Auditorium to the great singing palaces of the British Isles, but the Hilltoppers performed as though they were longtime veterans in the field. As the saying goes, even bad reviews are better than none at all. As the tour continued, and though the singers admitted to being homesick, they relished each and every opinion that was given of their performances.[25]

On the negative side was the *Evening Dispatch,* whose reporter said, "It is rather a pity that four talented young men should waste their time and the time of the greater part of the audiences, singing such banal, silly and sickly sweet songs as they did last night. No matter how bad modern popular lyrics are and no matter what kind of fans The Hilltoppers are trying to win, surely there must be songs less insulting to the intellect."

The reporter, frustratingly, did not identify the songs the Hilltoppers sang. They usually introduced their performances with "I Feel a Song Coming On," followed by "I've Got the World on a String," "Til Then," and other numbers with which they were identified. These songs were interspersed with Garvin's trumpet solos and Crowe's impersonations, in an effort to present a true variety show.[26]

Critics are apparently not held to the same standards as performers and writers. One must assume here that the old cliché applies: "Critics are frustrated authors and performers." Thus, their assessments must always be taken with the proverbial grain of salt. They are reactors rather than creators or doers.

A reporter for the *Edinburgh Evening News* said that the Hilltoppers looked "like four overgrown college kids dressed as if they had just stepped off campus." The negative tone of his subsequent review indicated that he probably intended this statement as disparagement; the truth was, however, he was right on the mark. They *were* "overgrown college kids" just off a campus. Jimmy Sacca, this obvious neophyte reported, "does not seem to enjoy himself" up there on the stage. Even after the Hilltoppers had been in England nearly a month, a reporter for the *Liverpool Evening Express* still referred to the W on Hilltopper sweaters as "unexplained." Apparently, many English and Scottish newspaper reporters were too embarrassed to ask what the W meant.[27]

"Oh, the illusion high pressure can cause," the *Evening News* reviewer started his report. While the Hilltoppers were "versatile" and "entertaining," they were no more talented than "lesser" groups "known on this side of the Atlantic." (To be sure, he did not identify any of the lesser ones he had in mind.)

The *Glasgow Herald,* speaking of the "red pullovers, open neck shirt, and white gym shoes," remarked upon "the military precision" of the Hilltoppers, with their advance and retreat on the stage, followed by the group's reforming around the microphone. All these maneuvers, said the reporter, actually helped communicate the "mournful emotionalism" that he thought was the Hilltoppers' message to the audience. That was, of course, only true for some of the Hilltoppers' songs, including "I'd Rather Die Young," "To Be Alone," and "My Treasure." The reporter missed the point: the Hilltoppers were love balladeers for the most part, at least at this stage of their career. While early rock 'n' roll was on the scene and the Hilltoppers had responded with "Do the Bop," it would take some time for rock 'n' roll to envelop the nation, to say nothing of the world.[28]

"Sing magnificently and look like a million" became the mantra for reviewers, except for the few who were obviously disaffected. Overwhelmingly, English reviewers and audiences loved the Hilltoppers; the naysayers, and any negative audiences, could, quite plainly, go to hell. The Hilltoppers were loved in England, and that's all there was to it. One reporter noted that the Hilltoppers were as popular in England as they were in America. They could have wandered onto the stage "from a football park," said one admiring reporter. "Variety at its best," reported the *Yorkshire Post,* "featuring the 'tight-lipped' Jimmy Sacca." (Of course, "tight-lipped" was not defined.) When it was announced that the Hilltoppers would extend their stay in the British Isles by at least two weeks, one magazine asked, "Who said variety was dead?"[29]

The *Manchester Evening News* said, "If you can bring yourself to imagine Johnny Ray split into four parts, you'll have a fair impression of the Hilltoppers." This was a compliment: the Hilltoppers had met Johnny Ray on numerous occasions and admired his talent and showmanship. "Agony," "exhilaration," and "tearful twisting of chords," according to this reviewer, were the trademarks of the Hilltoppers as they sang their ballads and love songs.[30]

"Toe-tapping rhythm, harmonizing, and jukebox rock 'n' roll are the group's specialty," reported another publication. There was a "masterly blending of voices" here, in an "almost caressing style." The Hilltoppers' recent release "D-A-R-L-I-N" was "clever stuff," said an English paper. "The Hilltoppers can still climb," another journal reported; "they're as nice as they sound." Their lyrics "meant something," their tunes were "slow and wholesome," and the four-square harmony behind "a sincere Jimmy Sacca" was popular not only with British audiences but with fans the world over. They were able to project all of the aspects of life—joy, love, hate, envy, pain, happiness—a great combination that helped Hilltopper publicity greatly.[31]

The Hilltoppers came to Britain in July 1956 and were supposed to leave in August. They didn't go home until September. Jimmy wrote a letter to *Hilltopper Topics* saying that out of the ten weeks they were in England, it rained for about nine. When the tour finally ended, most of the group took three-week vacations. Lou went to Greece, Eddie to Rome and France, and Karl traveled through Germany, France, and Italy. "They all had a great time," Jimmy reported.[32]

When the Hilltoppers returned to the States and to Western Kentucky Teachers College, they found significant changes. Acting on the 1954 and 1955 *Brown v. Board of Education* decision that public schools should be integrated "with all deliberate speed," Western admitted Margaret Munday, its first African American student. In contrast to some other places, this was done quietly, without fanfare, and without incident. When the singing Hilltoppers left for their foreign tour, Western was a segregated school; when they returned, it was integrated, and the group's members, like all other fair-minded people, were pleased at this development.[33]

As exhausted as they must have been when they reached Stateside, they nevertheless had a full schedule for the rest of the year. In the last three months of 1956, they performed well over twenty dates at colleges, ballrooms, and auditoriums and at military bases in Texas. In addition, they had full recording schedules and were special guests at many radio stations, particularly in St. Louis. Once again, they thrilled audiences at the Casa Loma (where there were so many encores that they quite literally ran out of songs), happily chatted with DJs Ed Bonner at KXOK and Chuck Norman at KSTL, and managed a guest appearance on local TV celebrity Gil Newsome's show. Also in St. Louis they sang at Jody's Restaurant and the Steeplechase Room of the prestigious Chase Hotel. The favorites of St. Louis audiences on these occasions were "I've Got the World on a String," "Time Waits for No One," "If I Didn't Care," "Poor Butterfly," "Love Walked In," and "Auld Lang Syne."[34]

On October 27, 1956, the Hilltoppers were in Memphis for a morning performance at Memphis State College's homecoming celebrations. That night, the Tigers played none other than the Hilltopper football team from Western Kentucky. (To the great delight of the home crowd, Memphis romped over Western, 42–0.) Directly after their performance in Memphis, they caught a plane to Carbondale, Illinois, to participate in homecoming celebrations (also on October 27) at Southern Illinois University, home of the Salukis. They joined Jaye P. Morgan and Buddy Mareno's Orchestra for two sold-out performances in Shyrock Auditorium. Throughout the day, at the National Guard Armory, one of their old friends, Johnny Long (whose most famous song was "Sailing Down the River on a Sunday Afternoon"), was entertaining large crowds with his orchestra. The Hilltoppers made a special appearance, primarily just to say hello, but they also had a "bang-up" time, as Jimmy announced their arrival by throwing a lit firecracker into the middle of the bandstand.[35]

But meeting with Long was not the most special event of the day. During one of their stints at Shyrock Auditorium a young man slipped in, as unobtrusively as he possibly could, and sat in the audience, greatly enjoying the concert. His name? Don McGuire! He was still in the army, stationed with an antiaircraft unit at a base in Baltimore, but had taken a weekend pass to St. Louis. He drove over to Carbondale to see his old buddies. "It was quite a reunion," *Hilltopper Topics* reported, for almost two years had passed since Don and Sy had put on Uncle Sam's uniforms. Don expressed great joy and said he was "very anxious" to rejoin the Hilltoppers, an event that was still a few months away.[36]

Just after their appearance in Carbondale, the Hilltoppers were booked in North Dakota. They did not make it to either the field house at the Agricultural College in Fargo or the Minot Municipal Auditorium. Instead, they were snowed in. In fact, they were stranded out on the highway and had to walk three miles to the nearest town where they found lodgings and working telephones. The two shows had to be canceled. When they finally got their car out of the North Dakota drift, they turned it south and headed for New Orleans and then to Houston.[37]

In the middle of January 1957, the group (still consisting of Jimmy Sacca, Eddie Crowe, Lou Mastor, and Karl Garvin) traveled to Winona, Minnesota, to be a part of the Winter Carnival. They gave two half-hour performances a day at St. Stan's Auditorium, to the delight of those in the jam-packed auditorium, who called for several encores at the end of each show.

On February 24, 1957, the Hilltoppers made another national television appearance, this time on *The Steve Allen Show.* The four came onto the stage wearing, not their trademark W sweaters and beanies, but identical fancy dinner jackets. Allen asked them if they had ever experienced "suppressed desires." Yes, they answered, they had. They explained that every time they appeared in public, they always wore matching clothes, and just once they'd like to "change and wear something different." Allen told them, "Go right ahead. Now's your chance." Each Hilltopper then proceeded to exchange jackets with another Hilltopper. Then, amid much applause from the audience, they temporarily retired from the stage.[38]

Appearing with the Hilltoppers were Brenda Lee, Yehudi Menuhin, Arlene Dahl, Aldo Ray, and Robert Ryan. The featured song on the program was a Hilltopper hit called "Marianne." Allen introduced it as "calypso," a form of singing, in his opinion, that was much better than the rock 'n' roll craze then becoming so popular throughout the country. Calypso always told a story, and it appealed not only to children but also to "mamas and papas," and that's why, he smilingly sang, he booked the "fabulous Hilltoppers."[39]

As a finale to the program, the other guests sang parodies

of "Marianne." Brenda Lee's parody expressed the age-old dictum that children should be seen and not heard. Menuhin sang about his violin performances at Carnegie Hall. Arlene Dahl serenaded "Fernando's Hideaway," to the tune of "Marianne." Aldo Ray sang in his parody that he owed his raspy voice to the fact that each day he gargled with ground-up glass. And, finally, Robert Ryan urged the audience to think of him as a "tough guy" only when he played the part in movies. The show closed with Allen, the Hilltoppers, and all the assembled guests happily singing "Marianne"—this time with the right words.[40]

Sales of "Marianne" shot up precipitously in the days following the Hilltoppers' appearance on *The Steve Allen Show.* Daily orders began to exceed twenty thousand records, so many that the staff at Dot had to work around the clock to fill them.[41]

Not long after the Allen show, an event occurred for which faithful fans around the world had been eagerly awaiting: the original Hilltoppers, with the exception of Billy Vaughn (who now lived in California), were back together! In early 1957, both Seymour Spiegelman and Don McGuire had completed their military duties and were discharged from the army. Their first stops were, of course, Moulton, Alabama, and Owensboro, Kentucky, to see their families. In mid-March 1957, the Hilltoppers were, for the most part, back together. The group was now made up of Jimmy Sacca, Eddie Crowe, Seymour Spiegelman, and Don McGuire. Though it meant losing their jobs, both Lou Mastor and Karl Garvin warmly welcomed Seymour and Don back into the fold. *Hilltopper Topics* gleefully reported on March 20 that "the Hilltoppers are back together for the first time since 1953," and already they were recording again, still with Dot Records. In these early moments of almost unbridled optimism, one fanzine said that "the original Hilltopper group" coming back together, "will have a definite effect on their popularity." Regrettably, only to an extent was this forecast borne out.[42]

Getting ready for their reentry into the Hilltopper orbit, both Don McGuire and Seymour Spiegelman wrote lengthy, heartfelt letters to their major fan magazine, *Hilltopper Topics*. Don said that even after a person's talents had gotten him into the world of entertainment, he must still "depend on a countless number of people to put his talents" across to the public. Fans are rarely if ever seen on TV or heard on radio, "but their contributions cannot be measured and the full gratitude which they greatly deserve can never be given."[43]

Seymour echoed these sentiments and added a personal note: not only was he once again a civilian, but he was also a brand-new father. His daughter's name was Penelope, or Penny, "and, of course, we think she's a little doll." He reminisced over the past five years, expressing wonderment that events had unfolded so quickly that "we were in some kind of daze." He thought back to the time when "Trying" was first recorded in Van Meter Auditorium. In thanking Hilltopper fans, Sy asserted, "If all the worldly things that being Hilltoppers has enabled us to acquire were taken away, we would still be left with some priceless memories." He knew, he admitted, that his letter was beginning to sound like a soap opera, "but I do mean every word."[44]

The first performance of the rejuvenated group was at Denver's famed hotel, the Brown Derby. Then they performed in the new high school gymnasium at Princeton, Indiana, on

March 28, 1957, where they were accompanied by the Jimmy Featherstone Orchestra. At a subsequent concert in St. Louis welcoming the Hilltoppers back, Don was so nervous that he knocked over the scenery. Longtime fan Carol Braddy exuberantly joined in the "Welcome Home" festivities in Bobbie Ann Mason's hometown of Mayfield. At a photo session, Carol's mother could not get both Carol and Jimmy in the viewfinder because Jimmy was so tall. He told Carol to put her arm around his neck. When she did, he straightened up and lifted Carol right off the ground, putting them both into the viewfinder. When they loaded their car (still a Cadillac) to go to another engagement, the trunk would not close because they had too much luggage. Seymour gleefully hopped up onto the trunk and jumped up and down on it, and he and Don pushed it shut.[45]

A few weeks later, the four again visited their fan club president, Bobbie Ann Mason, at her home in Mayfield, before an engagement in Paducah. Eddie Crowe spotted some horses in a nearby field. "I rode a horse once," he exclaimed. He said that he had said "120 words to it [and] 119 of them were 'whoa!'" Carol and Bobbie took the four shopping in Mayfield, where a local clothier donated a stage suit to each Hilltopper.[46]

These were happy days indeed, the first few weeks of the "new" Hilltoppers. One of their big hits at concert performances was "Ka-Ding-Dong," featuring this time the wonderful bass voice of Don McGuire. Each time McGuire sang the song, one of his three colleagues would slip up behind him and pull his pants legs well up above the knee, not only to show the song's intensity but also to delight the audience. The song dealt with a man smitten by a young lady and what it does to his heart.

The popularity of this "renewed" "Ka-Ding-Dong," with Don McGuire singing (he never did record the song) in person instead of Chuck Schroeder, justified the group's anger of the year before when Randy Wood had recorded the song using what many considered to be a bogus group of "Hilltoppers."[47]

Readjusting to the entertainment circuits and life on the road was once again the focus of these four young men. However, the Hilltoppers did not regain their pre-1956 popularity. The jukebox crowd that had loved them so much in the mid-fifties increasingly embraced rock 'n' roll. This was ironic, to say the least. "The Hilltoppers," argued one magazine, "more than any other white vocal group, gave unknowing glimpses into what form the traditional rock 'n' roll ballad" would become. Yet, it seemed that if their previous jukebox followers had not gone rock 'n' roll, they, as adults now, had opted out of music altogether. Thus, the Hilltoppers did not fit into any of the "oldies" formats: they found themselves in the late 1950s to be too young for adults and too old for kids. The group skidded from the hit parade to "the twilight zone," where "they were destined to remain in eternal limbo."[48]

Some musical analysts believed that as far back as 1952, the Hilltoppers could have won a permanent place for themselves in rock 'n' roll with their very first song, "Trying." If Billy Vaughn's piano playing for "Trying" had been "hard and choppy" instead of "detached and waltzy," "Trying" could very well have been the first rock 'n' roll ballad in the world. (This assessment was made after the fact, not before, making it more a statement of "what if" than a true analysis.) The Hilltoppers' recording of "Trying" was a full two years before "Earth Angel," by the Penguins, which got rock 'n' roll credit. (Generally,

Bill Haley and the Comets' 1955 recording of "Rock Around the Clock" is recognized as the first rock 'n' roll hit.) We must remember that the four original Hilltoppers came from barbershop, country, Italian operatic, and Jewish forms of music. Only the prescience of a soothsayer could have told the boys in 1952 what they had to do to stay popular, and it did no good in 1957 to keep reminding them of what might have been. Very few people in this world can escape the "what ifs" of life.[49]

But it was not just that the music genres changed so quickly that slowed the Hilltoppers rise. The Korean War with its military draft decimated the group. Sacca was drafted in 1953 and released in 1955, right when Spiegelman and McGuire were inducted, to stay in uniform for the next two years. There was no way the group's original exuberance could be maintained under these circumstances. Keeping the Hilltoppers together became too much a matter of going and coming. One can only wonder where the group would have gone if their careers had not been interrupted to such an extent. Altogether, during the life of the Hilltoppers, there were ten different members. One wag suggested that Dot Records send out four different groups, each equipped with one original member. This arrangement was, of course, unworkable.[50]

And, understandably, they wanted more time for their family lives. As noted before, they were all married, with growing children. Military service had necessarily kept them away from the family, and it was not easy to continue to be away on extended concerts. Thoughts of home certainly influenced the Hilltoppers and made them yearn for stability in their lives.

But the prediction that the Hilltoppers were heading into

"eternal limbo" was, happily, not entirely true. In fact, there were still many glory days—including more foreign tours—ahead of this group from Western Kentucky State College, and they made the most of them.

5 Hilltopper Tops

Here's a "letter" that showed up in one of the Hilltoppers' fanzines:

> "Sweetheart," "I Found Your Letter" on "This Stormy Night." "My Heart" went "Ka-Ding-Dong" when I saw your blue eyes "Crying in the Rain," and "Love Walked In." "I Can't Lie to Myself;" "Without You," "I'm Tormented," so "Can't We Try Again." "Darlin,'" "I'm Trying for Keeps," because "Until You're Mine," there will be "Teardrops In My Eyes." "You Made Up My Mind," "It's Only You," and I never want "To Be Alone." "If I Were King," "I'd Rather Die Young" because there is "No Greater Love," and "Time Waits For No One." "I'm So Tired" of "Searching" for "My Treasure" "Until The Real Thing Comes Along." "I'm Sending Bouquets And Kisses," and a "Faded Rose." "About a Quarter To Nine" we will "Do the Bop," to the "Kentuckian Song" and the "Old Cabaret." "Till Then." "Mary Ann" [departing from the usual spelling of "Marianne"] "P.S. I Love You."[1]

There were at least thirty-five Hilltopper recordings in this lineup. Letters such as this reflected the love and affection of fans all over the world. Many of these songs continued to play in the top ten of Hilltopper recordings. Of course, the first song to catch the public's attention was "Trying." Dot Records began to advertise this song in *Billboard* as early as May 1952 and, after the Sullivan show of October 1952, pushed it heavily. By late fall 1952, it was on *Billboard*'s Honor Roll of Hits. [2]

Billboard was founded in 1894 primarily to report on carnival entertainments around the country, but it ultimately changed to tracking popularity in music; hit record charts have existed since 1940. "To open a copy of *Billboard,*" said one author, "is to enter a space dominated by charts, numbers, hierarchies, predictions, and speculations." Coming out once a week, the magazine lists all of the most requested and played songs, based on DJ surveys and record sales; who sang them at what level of chart hierarchy (who is competing with whom); and how long each performer or group has been at a particular ranking; it also includes short articles about trends and other matters in the music industry. As one might expect, record companies advertised heavily in *Billboard,* touting their latest releases and saying why disc jockeys should play them.[3]

Billboard charts, as well as other musical journals, became an index of changing social ideas and practices in America, because of all the arts, music speaks most directly to the hearts of those listening. Popular lyrics comport with the mood of the time; only "the lyrics can turn a musical style into a movement." One can read back from the lyrics "the social forces that produced them." Time and again throughout both social and musical history, Americans have used lyrics to tell the world what's on their minds. From the 1950s to the present, musical lyrics have embraced complaints and protests against government authorities and their activities, against wars we thought unjust, against racism, and against poverty, among other things. "America is the home of an extraordinarily large group of musically innovative people. Clearly, Americans have a penchant for music and for inventing new forms of the art when its old forms . . . become inadequate in some way as vehicles for emotional and artistic expression."[4]

Certainly, the Hilltoppers were in the business of "emotional and artistic expression." November 1952 saw the release of "Must I Cry Again?" a song about losing one's lover and wishing her back. "Must I sigh again, must I cry again?" Jimmy Sacca sang in a pleading, even mournful, voice, making the listener sympathize with him and hope that his lost love will return to him. Would his former lover find a new interest? The song touched the nerves of any couple who had ever broken up, temporarily or permanently. No wonder it was listed by late December 1952, as a "best buy" by *Billboard* and other entertainment journals. By the close of the year, "Must I Cry Again?" was number 19 on *Billboard*'s Honor Roll of Hits, judged by DJs throughout the country.[5]

The momentum that started in 1952 made the Hilltoppers the number one singing group of 1953, a title bestowed by *Billboard, Cashbox,* the Juke Box Operators of America, record dealers, DJs, and, most importantly, fans. This honor was especially significant when one considers the able and popular Hilltopper competition. With groups like the Four Lads, the Four Freshmen, the Silhouettes, the Drifters, and other major groups of the day, the race for the charts was quite keen.

"If I Were King" hit the stands in February 1953 and almost immediately was dubbed as number four by jukebox operators, and then in a week or so, the song was elevated to number three. This song stayed high in all reporting agencies' charts throughout the entire year. "I'd Rather Die Young," which appeared in May 1953, was called by Dot Records and *Billboard* "the greatest record of our time." The song's popularity came as a pleasant surprise to the group. By May 25, 1953, it had risen to DJ popularity pick number three. (As noted earlier, the flip side, "P.S. I Love You," was number two and became the Hilltoppers' first million seller.) By August 1953, "I'd Rather Die Young" was one of the top ten songs performed on television on the numerous musical variety shows so popular at that time. (Generally speaking, viewing, listening, and reading audiences do not like the word "die" or "death" or even "tragedy" in whatever artistic offering comes before them. In an odd sort of way, however, "I'd Rather Die Young" was similar to a song performed many years later by George Jones, "He Stopped Loving Her Today." Both songs, despite their sad connotations, became runaway hits with listening audiences.)[6]

Jimmy Sacca went into the army in March 1953, but Randy Wood's foresight assured that there were two to three dozen Hilltopper recordings ready to be released at various intervals. This way, though the Hilltoppers performed few, if any, public concerts from March 1953 to March 1955, their records and jukebox offerings were kept before the American public. And the American public loved them. But the public also loved some other musical forms beginning to appear in the mid-1950s, rock 'n' roll being one of them.

Once, the Hilltoppers attended a Juke Box Operators of America convention, along with several other singing groups. Somewhat naively, Jimmy and his associates agreed to follow Mahalia Jackson onto the stage, after numerous other entertainers had declined to do so. Jackson chose her rendition of "The Lord's Prayer" for her contribution to the program. "Needless to say," Ann Sacca reported, "the Hilltoppers understood why nobody else wanted to follow her, so powerfully emotional was her performance." Of course, their reputation was not hurt by the incident; if anything, it was enhanced, because it showed the group's basic decency and good manners, and it helped them to go on to greater heights in the musical world.[7]

One of the joys of being the top performing group in the country is having not one but two, three, or even four records being presented to the American public at the same time, which allowed some competition among the songs, to see what fans liked the best. Of course, this was an enviable position. What singer or singing group would not have given their right arm for this kind of recognition in the musical world of the early 1950s—or, for that matter, at any time?

"To Be Alone" made the scene by September 1953. Many listeners quickly asked, Is it a religious song? A love ballad? It deals with the all-too-familiar story of lovers separating. But the dejected lover apparently finds strength in religion, for he falls on his knees and prays, and gets the message that it was meant for him to be alone. Don McGuire, to the accompaniment of organ music, gives a spine-tingling recitation of how he found comfort in meeting the destiny that had been laid out for him. Jimmy sings the lyrics, Don does the recitation, and Seymour and Eddie join in the harmony. It was a very effective and wonderful portrayal of the human condition.[8]

"To Be Alone," paired with "Love Walked In," at once became number six in record purchases in Cleveland; a week after its release, it was number one. Cleveland was a fairly accurate index to the rest of the country, for, many months after its release, "To Be Alone" continued to be described in all the entertainment magazines as "coming up in the trade."[9]

On into 1954, the Hilltoppers continued to enjoy encouraging statistics. A spate of songs was released by Dot Records and quickly became favorites among jukebox fans, radio listeners, and record purchasers. Throughout January and February, "To Be Alone," "Till Then" (also an Ink Spots song), "Time Will Tell," and "From the Vine" were the big Hilltopper hits. By midsummer, "Poor Butterfly" was "bustin' wide open." Throughout the country, fans were fascinated by Jimmy's "vowel explosions" and "aspirations" (discussed in chapter 2). The group began to receive "Hot Dots" from Dot Records—a type of special recognition for extraordinary performance—with each of their releases; this simply meant that Hilltopper songs quickly rose to the top in popularity in the United States.[10]

The transition from radio to television seemed to be nearing its completion during 1954, linking households in a common interest: entertainment. At the beginning of this transition around 1948, many, if not most, early TV shows were adapted from radio: *Amos 'n' Andy, Beulah, George Burns and Gracie Allen,* and others. In time, TV began to create its own programming. And so it was with much of the day's music. Radio and record producers still played and produced a variety of songs all the way from big band to pop music and emerging rock 'n' roll. If one record company had a significant hit, other large companies would release the same hit in a different format on its label "with their own singers or orchestras." This procedure generally eclipsed small, independent radio or recording groups who might have recorded the song in the first place. The biggest radio and recording groups in the three major genres of pop, country, and rhythm and blues were not interested in competition; on the contrary, they wanted to kill it. The producers and broadcasters of these genres were rather isolated from one another, and each offered its own variety of music.[11]

Randy Wood from Dot Records was one of the first entrepreneurs to take advantage of the practice of "covering" records, or recording material previously recorded by another artist. A cover was a "white cover" if the original version of the song had been recorded by a black group; many radio stations wouldn't play records by African Americans, which helped account for the popularity of white covers. Pat Boone became the poster boy for the cover practice, singing cover versions of rhythm and blues songs. Boone recorded a Fats Domino tune, "Ain't It a Shame?" He changed the title to "Ain't That a Shame," and, according to reports, if he had had his way, his version of the song would have been called "Isn't It a Shame?" Though he charted over sixty hits of his own for Dot (many of which were arranged by former Hilltopper Vaughn), Boone continues to be remembered as a cover artist. Other Dot singers who participated in the practice to a lesser extent than Boone were the Fontane Sisters, and Gale Storm; the Hilltoppers covered one song, "Only You." The cover practice eventually declined. The cover singers were fine and talented artists, but "the lack of original material" helped to lead to "their decline in the charts."[12]

Another factor that led to the demise of the cover practice was the creation of what became known as the Top 40. At lunch one day, the director of an Omaha, Nebraska, independent radio station became a bit annoyed when his waitress kept putting coins into the jukebox and selecting the same two songs over and over. It was her money, and it was the music that obviously she—and perhaps others—wanted to hear. The director reformatted his own offerings, "playing throughout the entire day, nothing but what the trade magazine charts showed were hit records." He changed the mix every week as soon as the new charts appeared, chiefly in *Billboard.* Thus was born the Top 40. By the end of 1954 and into 1955, the Top 40 concept had been picked up by radio stations all over the country. In a way the Top 40 format turned the radios of America into jukeboxes, a pleasing development for the Hilltoppers from Western Kentucky, since they had always been very popular with teenagers at the jukeboxes. At one time during this period, the group had eleven of the Top 40 hits being played on radio around the country. Like the cover songs, the Top 40 ran its course in a few years, and stations reverted to specialization in one genre or another.[13]

"Time Waits for No One" was the Hilltopper song that came out in late 1954. "It passes us by," intoned Jimmy's vibrant yet mournful voice, as he advised couples to love each other while they still had time. The other side of this record was "You Try Somebody Else," about sweethearts looking for the "real thing."

The Hilltoppers' old friend and partner Billy Vaughn was also flying high in the charts. He and his orchestra performed for an album, *Melody of Love* (an old Wayne King song), in December 1954, and early the next year, the album *Silver Moon* was issued. Billy appeared on the dust jacket of both albums, still wearing his beanie with a big W on it. He may have left the Hilltopper singing group, but his fondness for the group was still apparent.[14]

One of the biggest events of 1955 for the Hilltoppers (at this time made up of Jimmy Sacca, Eddie Crowe, Clive Dill, and Bob Gaye) concerned the popular movie *The Kentuckian,* starring Burt Lancaster. The Hilltopper song by the same name was the first recording since Jimmy got out of the army in March 1955. Everyone—and this most assuredly included the national fan club and its "territorial subsidiaries"—fervently hoped and believed that the Hilltopper sound track for the song would subsequently be used in the movie. Their dreams were realized, and the song was one of the featured parts of the movie. Jimmy felt that "The Kentuckian" would ultimately "be bigger than 'P.S. I Love You.'" His prediction here turned out to be incorrect. Country star Eddy Arnold, who also recorded "The Kentuckian," thought the Hilltoppers' version better. He took some people to his home to listen to the Hilltoppers sing "The Kentuckian."[15]

"The Kentuckian," who in the song "told the 'possum in the gumtree and the raccoon on the ground" about his love for his "darlin'," certainly did evoke images of rural Kentucky. In midsummer 1955, it was number ten among disc jockeys in Cleveland (many Kentuckians had gone to Cleveland and other parts of industrial Ohio during the war to find jobs; maybe this song made them homesick) and was described in *Billboard* and other entertainment journals as "coming up in the trade." As the movie went, however, so went the song. After the initial enthusiasm, the movie and record audiences turned to other interests.[16]

The next major recording was "My Treasure," which resonated with hundreds of thousands of couples around the world. It is about a man who has searched all his life for treasures of gold and for all the money his "pockets would hold." But then one day, looking into the mirror, he recognized what before he "never could see," that his greatest of treasures "was your love for me." This was very touching. What is a man's greatest treasure? More than gold and silver and material possessions, it is, quite plainly, his sweetheart or wife or life companion.

The fan clubs, both at home and abroad, quickly picked up on "My Treasure." One of the fanzines wrote: "You've surely heard the Hilltoppers' smash rendition of the beautiful ballad, 'My Treasure.' We're certain that it's 'your treasure' now." The flip side of "My Treasure" was a mambo tune, "The Last Word in Love." The national Hilltopper fan club, still headed by Bobbie Ann Mason, suggested that each member send requests to five different DJs asking them to play "My Treasure." They concentrated on Ed Bonner of St. Louis, Martin Block of New York, Howard Miller of Chicago, Jay Michael of Pittsburgh, and Bob Brown, of Newark, New Jersey. The strategy paid off, because "My Treasure" became immensely popular throughout the United States.[17]

In the trade surveys, *Billboard* listed "My Treasure" as the greatest Hilltopper hit so far in their career. It was number 61 out of the top 100; on the Honor Roll of Hits, it was number 12; on radio, it was number 38; and on TV, number 19. At this same time, the Hilltoppers' recording of "Only You" was well into its twenty-sixth week of being the best-selling pop record in the British Isles, although in the States, the Platters' recording of this song was higher on the charts than the Hilltoppers'—at least for a while. By February 1956 the Hilltoppers had overtaken the Platters, with the Hilltoppers at 42 out of the top 100, and the Platters trailing at 45.[18]

Next came "Eyes of Fire, Lips of Wine" and "I'm Walking through Heaven." Then, as has been noted before, Chuck

Schroeder and the G-Clefs became temporarily known as the Hilltoppers with "Ka-Ding-Dong" (see chapter 4). The Hilltoppers were in England when this recording came out. Apparently, there was a great deal of competition between the G-Clefs and the Diamonds with "Ka-Ding-Dong," with both versions staying in the top 100 popular songs in America. On September 15, 1956, the G-Clefs were at number 57, with the Diamonds trailing at 67. A week later, the G-Clefs remained somewhat steady at 56, but the Diamonds had risen to 50. These statistics must have given some comfort to the group from Western, who undoubtedly had been at least a bit miffed that Randy Wood had turned the G-Clefs into temporary Hilltoppers for the recording of "Ka-Ding-Dong." Perhaps this was why Dot advertisements in *Billboard* and other entertainment magazines began mentioning "The Towering Hilltoppers."[19]

One of the Hilltoppers' featured songs during their 1957 appearance on *The Steve Allen Show* was "Marianne." Its exposure to a national TV audience helped considerably to make it a countrywide hit. (The flip side was "You're Wasting My Time," with a different theme altogether from "Marianne.") Even children loved Marianne, the song said. If Marianne would marry her suitor, he would be friendly toward his mother-in-law. The song was done in a definite Caribbean style, which resonated with worldwide audiences. Dot's advertisements for "Marianne" in leading trade journals like *Billboard* and *Cashbox* used the original Hilltoppers in the photos. By February 16, 1957, the song was number 13 in the list of songs most played by jockeys throughout the country, number 19 for jukeboxes, and number 22 among best sellers in stores. As for sheet music, "Marianne" quickly became number 1 in Toronto and was by far the best selling in Great Britain. The Hilltoppers basked in their popularity in the British Isles, where fans made "Only You" the most popular song and "Marianne" their favorite sheet music.[20]

Then came an even greater success, "A Fallen Star." A "star fell from Heaven right into my arms," sings the lead singer, Jimmy Sacca. He concludes, "You must have strayed from the Milky Way," because a "falling star" is "what you are." Jimmy was never better with vowel explosions, or aspirations, adding "errr," "ahhh," and "huhhh," to the end of each measure. It was quite an effective device.

"A Fallen Star" was not a hit only for the Hilltoppers. Jimmy Newman recorded it, also on Dot; country music star Ferlin Husky recorded it on another label. For several weeks, there was practically a horserace among these three contenders with this beautiful song. By July 1957 the Hilltoppers' version of "A Fallen Star" was number 93 out of the 100 most popular songs in America; Husky's version was 85; Newman's was 43. A fortnight later, however, these statistics had changed. The Hilltoppers were 23, Husky 62, and Newman 47. These statistics seesawed back and forth for several weeks. One week Jimmy Newman was on top; another it was Ferlin Husky. The Hilltoppers' rankings were the most consistent of the three.[21]

After "A Fallen Star" came numerous Hilltopper songs that caught on with the jukebox crowd in the United States and with record buyers and sheet music aficionados. These songs included "My Cabin of Dreams" and its flip side, "Dedicated to You." In October 1957 the Hilltoppers came out with their recording of "The Joker." As stated before, this song was frequently compared to "The Great Pretender," by the Platters.

The Joker was a clown who put on a public persona but who inside was suffering heartaches. "The Joker is crying for you," Jimmy Sacca sings plaintively, showing once more that one's public face doesn't always match one's inner emotional state. The flip side of "The Joker" was "Chicken/Chicken," a frivolous song to balance the serious, somber, even heartbreaking, mood of the A side. "The Joker" stayed on the best-seller lists for several weeks in 1958.

The Operators Best New Releases for 1958 included the Hilltoppers' "You Sure Look Good to Me" and its flip side, "Starry Eyes." These songs did not go over well with the public, at least in terms of getting on best-seller lists. The Hilltoppers rerecorded "Trying," their signature song, as side B of "You're Nobody Till Somebody Loves You," but the recording received only a modest reception by the American listening public. In late August 1958 the Hilltoppers came out with "Peggy's Sister," with the flip side "Signorina."[22]

By early 1959 the Hilltoppers had recorded enough tunes for listening audiences to expect albums rather than just singles. The Hilltoppers tried to accommodate with a few albums that included the songs "I'd Rather Die Young," "Welcome to My Heart," "Lizzie Darlin'," and "Lots of Luck." By this time, however, the heyday of the Hilltoppers had passed, and they were struggling to stay alive in the minds of American and foreign publics. The military draft and rock 'n' roll had devastated them.

Their recordings ultimately reached a total of eighty. All of them were popular, especially among the hometown crowds in Bowling Green, Glasgow, and Hazard, Kentucky, and Lockport, and Seneca Falls, New York. They were heroes, no doubt about it. They had brought great credit not only to themselves but also to their hometowns and to Western Kentucky State College. Their overall national best-selling records were "P.S. I Love You" (over 3 million records sold), "I'd Rather Die Young" (1 million), "Marianne," (1 million), "Only You" (1 million), "Poor Butterfly," "To Be Alone," "The Joker," "The Kentuckian Song," "Love Walked In," "Trying" (1 million), " D-A-R-L-I-N," and "Till Then" (2.5 million).[23]

But their day had passed, although, in one form or another, the Hilltoppers lasted until at least 1963, mostly with their original members. After that, Jimmy Sacca attempted to keep his career alive, as he enlisted one singer after another in his group. For the most part, the original Hilltoppers passed into history, gaining the respect accorded to the past. This was nothing less than the original Hilltoppers deserve.

6 The Hilltoppers at Home and Abroad

If, as some reviewers had it, the Hilltoppers' fortunes were declining in the late 1950s, the group paid scant attention to them. Their performance schedules for the period of March–December 1957 were nothing short of amazing. One of the first to realize how busy the group would be was Bobbie Ann Mason, the national president of the Hilltopper fan club.

She thought it would be a swell idea for "the boys" to perform at her high school prom. After making her request, she heard from Randy Wood in January 1957 that he would try to arrange numerous engagements close to Bobbie's hometown. The letter stated, "You know the Hilltoppers will be delighted to appear for you." Unfortunately, it turned out to be impossible for the Hilltoppers to perform at the Mayfield prom. They had been booked at the Safari Room in New Orleans from May 16 through May 29. A Wood agent wrote, "Jimmy and the group were anxious to do this for you, to reciprocate for all your help and kindness to them."[1]

Another plan for the Hilltoppers that did not materialize—at least in 1957—was a second tour of the British Isles. The Hilltopper Fan Club of Great Britain reported in March that "the Hilltoppers will be over again for a tour of this island in

September." But, apparently, the long-awaited reunion of the group in March 1957 stimulated a huge number of recording sessions and personal appearances. It was not until the spring of 1958 that the Hilltoppers, this time with Don and Seymour, returned to the British Isles.[2]

Their Stateside engagements were still primarily between the Eastern Seaboard and St. Louis and Kansas City, Missouri. With Billy Vaughn and Randy Wood now in California, Hilltopper fortunes increased in the area west of the Mississippi River but not fast enough to overcome the rock 'n' roll craze beginning to sweep the nation. In fact, 1958 could very well have marked the turning point between "crooning," "balladeering," and rock 'n' roll.[3]

The Hilltoppers still had a great following, though. One fan in Hamburg, Illinois, noted how Jimmy's "dark eyes sparkled under the spotlight." And there was a fascination with a ring that Jimmy wore on the little finger of his left hand.[4]

The *Kansas City Star,* reporting on a Hilltopper concert, noted that the group seemed to be "in high favor with a great many adults" and "loved to pieces" by teenage girls. The group's love ballads had a "melting effect" on teenagers, the very kind of teenager who would rush to join a fan club after hearing the Hilltoppers perform. On this particular occasion in Kansas City, the Hilltoppers were singing in Eddie's Club, where it was difficult to get seats. The Hilltoppers were, reported an admiring local newspaper, "singers of melting ballads."[5]

The Hilltopper fan club of Kansas City hosted an afternoon picnic for "the guys," arranged by club president Peggy Sanford. They met in one of the city's parks and spent their time riding bicycles, eating hotdogs, and drinking colas. One feature that amused the Hilltoppers was a number of cupcakes with a large H worked into the frosting. One of the group, probably Seymour, pretended not to know what the H stood for.[6]

One of the big performance sites for the Hilltoppers in the fall of 1957 was the Michigan State Fair, in Detroit. Their song, "My Cabin of Dreams," with the flip side "Dedicated to You," had not been out long, and the fair was a great way to publicize the record and the group. Many Detroit-area disc jockeys had set up shop on the fairgrounds, and the Hilltoppers made the rounds, visiting and singing to each one. The disc jockeys included Robin Seymour, Don McCleod, and local TV personality Johnny Slagle. The Hilltoppers were guests on WXYZ-TV's *Dance Matinee* and also on the TV show of another local celebrity, Soupy Sales.[7]

Bobbie Ann Mason traveled 750 miles to be on hand for all the personal appearances and performances at the Michigan State Fair, where she was joined by Millie Hovizi of Ferndale, Michigan. Mason was accompanied by Jo White, Detroit Hilltopper fan club president, and Margie Gluth, also from Ferndale, to work to obtain the largest possible entertainment exposure for their favorite singing group. Mason noted that, while in Detroit, Jimmy traded in the "old" blue Fleetwood Cadillac (two years old) for a brand-new, shiny black 1957 model. (After all, what else is one to do in Detroit?) There was only one disappointment with the Hilltopper appearances in Detroit: they had been scheduled to appear on Alan Freed's show, *The Big Beat,* but the program was canceled.[8]

While in Detroit, the Hilltoppers wrote a letter (probably penned by Seymour Spiegelman) to all their fans. They mentioned that they were appearing at the fair with Johnny Ray, Bill

Haley and the Comets, the Tyrones, the Rhythm Kings, Sammy Shore, and Edye Gorme. This all-star lineup was enough to make their heads spin, especially since the group was only a bit over five years old.[9]

They were on the road too much in the latter part of 1957 to "call any place home." Nevertheless, they still had contacts with the outside world, so to speak, and expressed their thoughts about some of the popular cultural life in the United States. They saw movies whenever possible. Seymour's favorite was *Twelve Angry Men,* starring Henry Fonda, Lee J. Cobb, and an all-star cast. Jimmy said he thought TV "today is better than ever, with such a vast choice of programs among education, musicals, varieties, Westerns, and comedies." He was particularly fond of performances by Sid Caesar. Eddie liked TV Westerns but was worried that "overexposure" might cause all of them to wane in public popularity. He joined millions of other Americans who objected to the networks' practice of putting on the most popular shows exactly opposite each other. "To get perfect TV" and eliminate so much "channel changing," Eddie presciently remarked, "we will see the innovation of Pay TV." Don liked *Playhouse 90* and joined all three of his comrades in the thought that *Gunsmoke* should win an Emmy, if for nothing else than the "offbeat character" of Chester, played by Dennis Weaver.[10]

Their families continued to grow throughout 1957. Terry Randolph Sacca, Jimmy and Ann's second son, was born, and Jimmy started going around "armed and dangerous" with photos. (If Terry had been a girl, according to reports, his parents would have named him Susan.) To the amusement of an audience in Kansas City, Jimmy demonstrated how to fold and put on a diaper, using a table napkin for the occasion. Seymour's daughter, Penelope, was growing rapidly, while Don McGuire and his wife, Maxine, soon became proud parents for the second time with the birth of Kreis in February 1957. The very next month, Don rejoined the Hilltoppers, and it did not take him long to get back into "the old groove." Still, he said, the "hardest part I've found in this business is leaving Maxine, my wife, and our two children." Being away from them while they stayed behind in Owensboro, he said, "really hurts when . . . I leave for weeks at a time." During the next two years, things did not improve in this respect, as literally hundreds of performances, both at home and abroad, lay before them.[11]

The year 1958 opened for the Hilltoppers with great excitement about their return trip to the British Isles and various other parts of Europe. *Hilltopper Topics* exuberantly reported the upcoming ten-week tour, hoping that "Big Ben [would tick] in time to their music." They left in early April for an eight- or ten-week tour, depending on their reception, of Britain and other parts of the European continent. Before leaving New York they saw the rehearsal for Pat Boone's *Chevy Showroom* and were thrilled to make the acquaintance of boxer Rocky Graziano and entertainer Pearl Bailey. On the way to Britain they stopped in Newfoundland for refueling. Their initial engagements were in Newcastle, Leeds, Glasgow, Edinburgh, Liverpool, Manchester, Bristol, Sheffield, and London. As in 1956, they were "wonderfully" and "most warmly" received by audiences who certainly remembered their previous performances. They received glowing reviews from the *South Yorkshire Times,* the *Manchester Evening Chronicle,* Bristol's *Western Daily Press,* the *Bristol Evening World,* and the *Sheffield Star.* Some newspapers reported that during one of the Hilltopper performances, a little black puppy wandered into the theatre and marched right up to the stage. Many in the audience thought this was part of the act, but it wasn't. The Hilltoppers temporarily adopted the mutt and took it to some of their other concerts where, every time it appeared, "the crowds went wild." There was no subsequent report on what happened to the puppy.[12]

But the attention and questions from the press seemed to differ considerably from just twenty-four months earlier. In 1956, reporters wanted to know about the Hilltoppers' place in the musical world and how they coped with it. They emphasized Hilltopper singing styles, especially that of Jimmy Sacca, and how the Hilltoppers felt they compared with up-and-coming rock 'n' rollers like Bill Haley, Fats Domino, Buddy Holly, and above all Elvis Presley. In 1956 their music was still very much in vogue; it was still in vogue in 1958 but not quite as much.[13]

British reporters in 1958 were apparently more interested in Hilltopper cultural and political views of the world than anything to do with music. For example, the Hilltoppers opined that the British were "behind" in such things as home furnishings, clothing styles, and cooking abilities. On the other hand, the British were "1,000 times" more sensible than Americans in medical and dental programs. Citizens paid something like $50 a year to the government, which then saw to it that they had medical and dental work free of charge. "It certainly is something we can look at and envy." What was the British attitude toward American entertainers? the reporters also asked. "Fond of the good ones," the Hilltoppers replied. "At least, they were able to tolerate us!" They came into contact with several American performers touring Britain at the time: Johnny Ray, Sarah Vaughan, Charlie Gracie, Johnny Puelo, and James Melton.[14]

Their sightseeing included Buckingham Palace, the Tower of London (where they pronounced the Crown Jewels the most impressive exhibit in all of England, and their favorite), Trafalgar Square, St. Paul's Cathedral, and the execution scaffolds of Anne Boleyn and Katherine Howard, two wayward wives of Henry VIII back in the sixteenth century. They loved British live entertainment, such as *My Fair Lady, Expresso Bongo, The Party,* and *No Time for Sergeants.* But they loathed British television. It was "terrible" compared to American TV, primarily because there was only one channel, the BBC. True, "telly" was government controlled and there were no commercials, but you still had to pay a rather hefty license fee to play it legally in the privacy of your home. Also, British television tended to copy programs that had originated in the United States. "For each of our top ranking shows, there is an English version."[15]

There were few cars in England (and these were small by American standards), the Hilltoppers observed, remarking on the number of bicycles in use. Most Englishmen could not afford to travel by plane. Though they were enchanted by England and loved their fans, when asked how they felt about returning home, their answer was, "Oh man, there's nothing like it." Quite clearly, the Hilltoppers were homesick. A reporter for the *Liverpool Evening Express* visited the group in their hotel just before a performance. Seymour told him, "I am homesick all the time." Don McGuire, waving a letter he had just received from his wife, remarked, "This is the nicest thing that can happen to a guy away from home."[16]

That the reporters did not concentrate on their singing performances probably indicated that the Hilltoppers were not as popular in England in 1958 as they had been two years before. Things had changed, and not to their liking or benefit. There were signs throughout the United States that said "Elvis for President," and this thought had made its way to the British Isles. And, though the Hilltoppers' "Do the Bop" was something of a tribute to rock 'n' roll, it just didn't work. They were forever identified as "love balladeers" and not associated with rock 'n' roll. This identification hurt their latter-day image. When Elvis was drafted into the U.S. Army in the early sixties, one reporter remarked that "national service" had robbed America of its leading teen hero only for two years, but "two years in pop was a lifetime." If anyone realized the truth of this statement, it was the Hilltoppers from Western Kentucky State College.[17]

If the original Hilltoppers had stayed together as a group, things might have turned out differently. But the draft cut into the careers of these young performers, just as later it did Elvis's. The Korean War was on, and government priorities prevailed. There was no discernible bitterness among the Hilltoppers because of their service to Uncle Sam; nevertheless, the draft kept a great many things from happening with many musical groups.

The Hilltoppers rerecorded "Trying" in 1958, in an effort to increase their lagging popularity. " But, even if the reissued version had been redone in rock 'n' roll style, with a choppier piano accompaniment, rather than the flow with which Billy Vaughn had originally arranged it, it most likely would have made no significant difference.[18]

A second factor in the group's waning popularity was

that the music-loving public went through many stages when they didn't know who the Hilltoppers really were. At least ten people became "singing Hilltoppers." Of course, British audiences, generally speaking, did not know the original makeup of the Hilltoppers, but they loved them anyway. There were some who read newspapers and the reviews therein and asked questions about this group from a small educational institution in Bowling Green, Kentucky.

And third, the sales of their records were declining, a situation that is almost always a kiss of death for recording artists. "We got used to having million sellers [records] until we finally made one that dropped to half a million," Jimmy Sacca told a reporter. "We thought that was just a fluke," he continued, "but the next one dropped to 250,000, and then to 100,000, and then we were dead." Of course, they were nowhere near dead; it was all a matter of comparison.[19]

After the 1958 tour in England, they came back to Kentucky and opened their Stateside engagements with performances at Louisville's Iroquois Gardens. As perhaps a sign of the times, the group arrived in a Chevrolet station wagon rather than the usual Cadillac. In fact, Jimmy gave the Cadillac to his wife, Ann, while the group settled for less comfortable traveling quarters. They performed "Sugartime," which had been popular in the British Isles, and "When the Saints Go Marching In," featuring Eddie Crowe on the trumpet, as well as "Laugh, Clown, Laugh." Eddie's impersonations, always enjoyable, became even more so when he added Clark Gable to his repertoire.[20]

After their appearances in the Iroquois Gardens in July, the Hilltoppers essentially made one-night stands for most of the remainder of the year. They went to Houston, where, at the Tidelands Motor Inn, they were on the same ticket with comedian Jonathan Winters. Don McGuire was especially pleased when he learned that Winters not only knew of Hazard, Kentucky, Don's hometown, but had been through it on several occasions. Winters said he used to drive a semi from Hamilton, Ohio, through Hazard, on his way to a Standard Oil station in Jenkins, Kentucky. One night during their stay in Houston, famed baseball player Stan Musial came up onto the stage, to the delight of the audience.[21]

They also benefited from surveys and profiles by local fan clubs of significant disc jockeys in the United States and Canada. Their close friend Peggy "Dixie" Sanford made Vic Kearns of Kansas City's KUDL an honorary member of the Hilltopper fan club. Kearns had met the singers and said that they "deserved all the credit" for being "one of the top vocal groups in the country." Millie Hovizi did a profile of DJ Ron Knowles of station CKLW in Windsor, Ontario, whose show was "quite popular" among Detroit audiences. "Ron," Millie reported, "thinks highly of 'the boys,' and has promoted their records and the [fan] club a great deal." Shirley Mero of Worcester, Massachusetts, profiled a local celebrity, Paul Larson, who said that the Hilltoppers sing "sensible songs" and that "you can understand the story that they are trying to put across to their fans." The Hilltoppers obviously enjoyed the songs they either recorded or sang in public.[22]

In early December 1958, they literally "slipped in and out of Bowling Green." They used the Music Building on the Western campus to rehearse for an upcoming concert appearance in Birmingham, Alabama. On campus, they had "no idea" that the present Western student body would be "so wild about them." Each time they walked over to the Music Building to practice, at least sixty to seventy students "crowded into the room to listen to the singing." When they walked around the campus of their alma mater, they were besieged by hundreds of admiring students looking for handshakes, photos, and autographs. To be sure, the boys didn't mind one bit. They were used to admiring crowds, but these students were their own, and it was a love affair from the beginning. It would have been difficult to overstate their popularity on campus. The Hilltoppers were to perform before an appreciative audience at Birmingham-Southern College.[23]

By the time of the Birmingham concert, the Hilltopper personnel had once again changed, and the rehearsals at Western were as much to introduce their new member to the group as it was to perfect their singing styles. Eddie Crowe decided that it was time for him to strike out on his own, and he tendered his resignation, affirming that his affiliation with the Hilltoppers had "been happy and educational." He was almost immediately booked at the Bambau Room of the Town House Motel in Monroeville, Pennsylvania, an engagement that kept him busy until at least the midway point of 1959. Interestingly enough, Town House management scheduled another act at the Bambau Room, in addition to Eddie Crowe. They were the Hilltoppers! "What a reunion!" exclaimed one person when Eddie and the Hilltoppers simultaneously converged on the stage. Apparently, neither Eddie nor the Hilltoppers knew that this would happen. They sang far into the night, reminiscing and reflecting upon the world and their place in it.[24]

Eddie's replacement was Douglas Cardoza, of Tulare, California. He was a Western student, a music major, and the brother-in-law of Seymour Spiegelman. It was his talent in singing, and only his talent in singing, that got him a slot in the Hilltoppers. Immediately after he graduated from high school, Cardoza had joined the U.S. Navy and served four years in its bands. At Western, he was active in the Red and White Dance Band. "Addition of Cardoza to the group," an admiring local columnist wrote, "means that every member of The Hilltoppers is once again either a graduate or former student of Western."[25]

Directly after the Birmingham concert, the Hilltoppers once again began packing their bags. They were heading back to Europe, this time not to the big pleasure palaces of the British Isles but to the nightclubs, private clubs, and U.S. military bases in Germany and France. Why not the big venues? "For one thing," said Jimmy Sacca, "we did not [at that time] have a number one record." It was the same old story: an author is known only by the success of his last book, singing groups only by their most recent hit.[26]

The Hilltoppers sang their way through Germany and France during the closing days of 1958, but on the whole the experience was unfulfilling and certainly some kind of catalyst that caused at least one of the group to make a basic, life-changing decision. They performed for private parties, nightclub audiences, and military officers—French, German, and American—at numerous bases. They were aware that they could make a lot of money in European nightclubs, some of which closed at midnight, and some that never closed. In addition, the numerous U.S. military bases offered great economic opportunities for singing groups. The Hilltoppers were not performing because of any audience love, on the part of either the Hilltoppers or the concertgoers, but because they had been hired to entertain specific groups.

This situation did not sit at all well with the Hilltoppers. They were still young men, not yet out of their twenties, and they were homesick, especially with Christmas being so close. Also, they were balladeers, and often their audiences wanted rock 'n' roll. Nevertheless, the group managed to sustain themselves through France and Germany during the Christmas season of 1958.

But such an existence exacted a price. "We were in Mannheim, Germany, at Christmas 1958," reported McGuire, "and we had to drive down to France in a little bus for a job, and they were doing two of these a day." The driver, Fritz Falkenrack, who was also their pianist, got them out on the autobahn, heading for their next engagement, "and we looked at each other," and exclaimed, "It's Christmas!" Some three thousand miles away from home, in a "little old place in France," Don McGuire remembered, "and my wife and children were in Owensboro, Kentucky!" None of the Hilltoppers had a reputation for drinking, but when their bus passed by a local bar or bistro, they asked Falkenrack to stop. They went in and got "stinko." That's the way they celebrated Christmas 1958.[27]

At the end of this tour, Jimmy Sacca promised himself that he would never sacrifice another Christmas with his family. Don McGuire, arriving home in Owensboro, found that his young daughter, Lisa, didn't know him. She scratched at him and pushed him away. Another daughter applauded in her sleep. Both Jimmy and Don drew inferences from these experiences. Their families needed them, and they most assuredly needed their families. Though the Hilltoppers kept singing long after the Christmas 1958 tour, it became increasingly clear to all of them that home life was preferable to hundreds of one-night stands. At the very least, they were now determined, there would be no more Yuletides away from their wives and children.[28]

Though their musical style was said to have been losing popularity (in favor of rock 'n' roll and bebop) one would not have known it by looking at the Hilltoppers' schedule for the first part of 1959. Refusing to spend another Christmas abroad certainly did not mean a curtailment of activities at home. They played Roy Colombo's Club in Chicago as the new year opened, followed by the Officers' Club at Schilling Air Force Base in Salina, Kansas. They went on to Rockhurst College in Kansas City and then to engagements in Topeka, Kansas, and Springfield, Missouri. Other venues for the first three months of 1959 included St. Louis; Memphis; Mount Pleasant, Iowa; Rockford, Illinois; Milwaukee and Waverly City, Wisconsin; and Southeastern Louisiana State College in Hammond, Louisiana, with Ralph Flannigan's Band. They sang at Miami University of Ohio with the Glenn Miller Orchestra, then at Granville, before ending up in Springfield, Ohio, with the Jimmy Dorsey Band.[29]

Then they came back to their mecca, Western Kentucky State College. In May 1959 they returned for a wonderful concert in Van Meter Auditorium, where it had all started. To the thorough delight of their audience made up of students and faculty, the Hilltoppers sang "If I Didn't Care," "To Be Alone" (featuring the solo narrations of Don McGuire), and "The Kentuckian." They were on their way to Lima, Ohio, for another performance and were looking forward to the upcoming college season, during which they were to sing at numerous institutions of higher education in Ohio and throughout the country. The Hilltoppers were always popular with the college crowd; there was an immediate rapport between the group and students. This happy relationship, of course, was not hard to explain: the Hilltoppers had been students when they started out in 1952, and in more ways than one they always remained students. As one newspaper and magazine article after another reported, they were "at heart, still teenagers" themselves.

In the middle of the year, they were on their way to the Far East for an extensive performing tour. Billy Vaughn and his orchestra had become popular in Japan and other places in the Orient. It was therefore just a matter of time until the Hilltoppers were invited to perform their magic on "the mysterious East." The headliner was Neil Sedaka, but the Hilltoppers were right behind him at the Arenata Coliseum in Manila, the Philippines, (where, later, the "thrilla from Manila" was fought between Louisville's Muhammad Ali and Joe Frazier) with audiences of twenty-five thousand each night. They stayed in the Philippines for a fortnight and then moved on to Japan, where, among other places, they performed at Sangyo Bunka Kai Kan in Kawasaki City and at the open-air concert hall, Hibiya Yagai Ongakudo, in Tokyo. They were so popular in Japan that for nearly two months a local TV station asked the Hilltoppers to host their own television variety show. They recorded some of these shows in advance so they could perform at other places. Their travels to Okinawa must have brought back some memories (fond or otherwise) for Jimmy Sacca, who had been stationed there in the army six years before. They went on to Formosa (Taiwan) and other places in the Far East, such as

South Korea (where they gave several concerts at Seoul City Auditorium) before returning home. It was an intriguing tour, heady, but only to some extent fulfilling. The Hilltoppers by now had been performing for seven years, but they could just as well have been beginning. It was analogous to the worker who has to "reinvent the wheel" every time a new bureaucrat comes along. "Who *are* you?" began to prey upon the minds of people who bought records. Nevertheless, the Hilltoppers persevered.

Back in the States in the summer of 1959, the Hilltoppers were booked for a performance in Altamont, Illinois. One of the regional Hilltopper fan club presidents, Carol Braddy, was in attendance. The club where they were to perform was just across the road from a racetrack. Don McGuire asked whether they had "car races or trotters" there. Braddy didn't know because she had never been there before. Don "took a deep breath and said, 'Must be trotters. Hot rods don't smell like that.'"[30]

Though they were of good cheer, the four could sense changes ahead. And so could their national fan club president, Bobbie Ann Mason. She and some friends drove from Lexington, where she was a student at the University of Kentucky, to Louisville, to see the Hilltoppers in a concert headlined by the "velvet fog," Mel Torme. She sat at a table with Don and Seymour and apologized for the newsletter being two months late. Don told her, "It's about time you forgot about the fan club. . . . People change and go on to something else. . . . We won't stay with this forever. It's no way to live—one dinky ballroom after another. Travelling around all the time isn't what it's cracked up to be."[31]

"Even in a Cadillac?" Bobbie Ann asked. "Even in a Cadillac," Don replied somberly.[32]

Even after Mel Torme had completed his repertoire, the crowd continued to go wild. Jimmy Sacca took the microphone and sang "I Can't Get Started," and then "he eased into 'St. James Infirmary,'" which Bobbie Ann characterized as the "meanest, low-downest, saddest song I ever heard. I thought I would die. It was after hours, way down South in Dixie. It was 1959."[33]

If the conversation with Bobbie Ann was not a swan song for the Hilltoppers, it certainly was prescient. Don McGuire was the first one to leave. His three children were growing up without him, and he increasingly yearned for a family life. The group performed at a supper club in Wisconsin in early 1960, and afterward Don took off his tuxedo, shoes, and makeup and announced his retirement. "You can never get all the makeup off," he said metaphorically. "It stays with you."[34]

His brother, Bobby, who now lived in Atlanta, worked with the publishing company of Holt, Reinhart, and Winston, and he recommended Don to another publisher, Harcourt, Brace, and Jovanovich. Don said later, "I thought they sold braces." He told Bobby that he had had a "wonderful eight years" with the Hilltoppers but it was time to move on to something else. He met with the Harcourt, Brace representatives in Louisville and embarked on a new career, which opened up vistas for him that he had never before imagined. "You have to know what's in those books," he said, so "you have to read them all." He began to receive a brand-new education from selling textbooks. One of his first clients was superintendent of a Western Kentucky school system who chewed Red Man and spat in a spittoon and kept trying to get Don to take a "chaw." After a year or so, Don did; "I made myself used to it." No matter what he had to do to make sales, at least one thing was sure: he was home now with his wife and children every day, and loving every minute of it. He never forgot that he had been a singing Hilltopper, but he now thoroughly savored life as an everyday citizen.[35]

In the meantime, Jimmy, Seymour, and Douglas did everything they could to keep the group together as a trio, getting engagements at various places. But it just wasn't the same. Moreover, Jimmy, the lead singer, had begun having trouble with hoarseness as early as 1956—almost always ultimately a fatal blow to the career of a singer. (Physicians found nodules on his vocal cords and told Jimmy that surgery was the only option. The surgery was performed in Los Angeles, and it was successful, but Jimmy had had to refrain from talking, let alone singing, for at least four months.) Eventually, the three gave up the effort and moved in different directions.[36]

Seymour, hoping for the time the Hilltoppers would once again get back together, went to work as a distributor for Dot Records in Memphis. Douglas decided to go back to Tulare, California, where for some time he worked at a bar. Then he became a telephone lineman.[37]

Jimmy became a branch manager for Dot Record Distributors in Buffalo, Philadelphia, and New York City. In 1963 he moved to Jackson, Mississippi (his wife, Ann, was originally from the Magnolia State), where for a year or so he worked with Ace Records Distributors. In 1964 he opened a restaurant and became one of Jackson's best-known restaurateurs, and he also took on a job as the southeastern representative for a company called National Educational Consultants. It was a living, but Jimmy Sacca didn't like it. After some time, he decided to put together another singing group. Its name? The Hilltoppers, of course.

Seymour Spiegelman moved to New York and was a regional distributor for some time for Dot Records there. He and his wife, Jeanne, continued to take pride in their family and also wrote children's songs and stories (they were still collecting royalties as late as 2006). Eddie Crowe continued to perform not only at the Bambau Room in Monroeville, Pennsylvania, but also in numerous other entertainment spots, especially throughout the eastern United States. Karl Garvin, who had played the trumpet so brilliantly for the Hilltoppers, landed a job in the band that provided the background in all of Pat Boone's performances.[38]

Were the original Hilltoppers happy in their new situations? This question, of course, is not easily answered, because "happiness" is interpreted in so many different ways. Our lives are not either this or that. There are a lot of in-betweens. It is possible for a person to be happy and sad at the same time. It is certain that Don McGuire, Seymour Spiegelman, and Jimmy Sacca, all family men by the opening years of the 1960s, were happy primarily to be at home with their wives and children, even though this meant working at occupations that had nothing to do with music making. At the same time there were the memories. It was, as Don McGuire had said, "hard to get all the makeup off." It stayed with you, always.

The Hilltoppers in the late fifties and early sixties were not quite finished. There were some performances ahead, and not only with Sacca's revival of the group. In 1972 they participated in an emotional homecoming at Western Kentucky University, where they performed several songs. It was clear that if the Hilltoppers were no longer together as a group, they lived on in the memories of thousands of people.

The Hilltoppers, ca. 1952. From top clockwise: Jimmy Sacca, Seymour Spiegelman, Don McGuire, Billy Vaughn. (Bruno of Hollywood; WKU archives.)

The Hilltoppers performing at Van Meter Auditorium, probably 1953. From left to right: Seymour Spiegelman, Jimmy Sacca, Billy Vaughn, Don McGuire. (Moss Photo, New York; WKU archives.)

Western Kentucky University homecoming, 1972. From left to right: Seymour Spiegelman, Billy Vaughn, Jimmy Sacca, Don McGuire. (Robert K. Stuart; WKU archives.)

Toast of the Town, October 26, 1952. (WKU archives.)

Private First Class Jimmy Sacca in 1953 after he became one of Uncle Sam's own. (Carl E. Janusek; WKU archives.)

Poster of the 1958 tour in England. (Photo by the author, courtesy of Don McGuire.)

Cartoon of the Hilltoppers as they embarked on their 1956 tour of England. From left to right: Eddie Crowe, Jimmy Sacca, Lou Mastor, Karl Garvin. (Sacca Collection.)

The Hilltoppers, October 26, 1952. From left to right: Jimmy Sacca, Don McGuire, Ed Sullivan, Randy Wood, Billy Vaughn, Seymour Spiegelman. (WKU archives.)

The Hilltoppers, ca. 1952. From left to right: Don McGuire, Seymour Spiegelman, Randy Wood, Jimmy Sacca, Billy Vaughn. (Sacca Collection.)

The Hilltoppers' name on the marquee in New York, one of many on which it appeared during their career. (Courtesy of Jimmy Sacca.)

(Above) Don McGuire and two of his most devoted fans, March 28, 1957. From left to right: Carol Braddy of Mount Vernon, Illinois; Don McGuire; and Bobbie Ann Mason, of Mayfield, Kentucky, the first president of the national Hilltopper fan club, who went on to become a world-famous author. (Courtesy of Carol Braddy.) *(Below)* Getting ready for a concert, in front of Bobbie Ann Mason's house, May 6, 1957. From left to right: Seymour Spiegelman, Don McGuire. (Courtesy of Carol Braddy.)

Teen O'Clock Time with the Hilltoppers at KMOX radio in St. Louis, Missouri, the Hilltoppers' home away from home. From left to right: unknown, Jimmy Sacca, Seymour Spiegelman, Don McGuire, unknown. (Edward H. Goldberger, St. Louis; WKU archives.)

Despite their smiles, both Bobbie Ann Mason and Jimmy Sacca knew that the Hilltoppers were on their way to becoming just a treasured memory. This photo was probably taken shortly before Mason enrolled in the University of Kentucky, in Lexington.

The "Hub of the Hill," the Goalpost, where Western Kentucky State Teachers College students went for hamburgers and music, and where the Hilltoppers began to perform in the early 1950s. Owners Hubert and Gladys Greer offered food and drink on credit to numerous students, which probably encouraged attendance at performances and hence boosted the Hilltoppers' popularity. (WKU archives.)

Veteran Hilltoppers. From left to right: Billy Vaughn, Jimmy Sacca, unknown, Seymour Spiegelman, Don McGuire. (Photo by Dan Jackson; Sacca Collection.)

Staying in shape on their 1956 English tour. From left to right: Unknown, Lou Mastor, Karl Garvin, Jimmy Sacca, Eddie Crowe, Colin Grainger (?). (Sacca Collection.)

Among admiring fans, ca. 1953, shortly after Jimmy Sacca went into the service. Bottom row, from left to right: Don McGuire, Jimmy Sacca, Seymour Spiegelman, Billy Vaughn. (Photo by Dan Jackson; Sacca Collection.)

The Hilltoppers scattered around a room full of ardent admirers, ca. 1953. Seymour Spiegelman, Don McGuire, and Billy Vaughn are wearing the W beanies. (Sacca Collection.)

Gold record of "P.S. I Love You." (Photo by the author, courtesy of Don McGuire.)

"We were running the label in the record shop; this company was one desk in the corner of Polly's office — that was Dot Records."

Dot Records

Varese Vintage – Preserving the Sounds of Dot Records

By John Michlig

Rock music historians are of nearly one mind when the subject of Pat Boone's singing career comes up. A refrain especially prevalent among the more caucasoid of writers is that Boone's whitebread R&B covers served to overshadow the performances of Black composers who originally recorded the songs; the non-white versions could get no airplay, it was reasoned, because "safe" and sanitized teen idols were co-opting the songs (if not the vibe). This is a righteous opinion that I myself parroted at many a beer keg, meanwhile rooting posthumously for Alan Freed, a disc jockey known to rock history as a hero and major proponent of the "raw, original, off-the-street" wax: the anti-Boone. Hey, kids — here's the real thing!, he screamed into a microphone at WABC. Here, kid — let me sign that publishing contract with you!, he brayed at Chuck Berry. In retrospect, one can't help but agree that "royalty split" is a concept a bit more malign than "white cover version."

Ethics aside, the simple fact is that Freed's Moondog Matinee didn't reach my parents' Philcos. My clear recollections of my mom singing "I Hear You Knocking" in the finely enunciated style of Gale Storm is due to her teen collection of well-worn, parent-approved Dot Records. Black R&B could enter midwestern households through the front door in only this way. "Tutti Frutti" would've never been heard at all without the Boone smile and Dot label behind it. Recently, Varese Vintage has made available CD collections of '50s to mid-'60s artists on Dot Records, a label that lead the pack in purveying flawless, smooth and utterly mainstream pop confections in the dawn of rock and roll. Now available: *Pat Boone: More Greatest Hits, Dark Moon: The Best of Gale Storm, Melody of Love: The Best of Billy Vaughn, Hearts of Stone: The Best of The Fontane Sisters,* and *P.S. I Love You: The Best of The Hilltoppers featuring Jimmy Sacca.*

"In the '50s there were a lot of white artists covering black R&B songs, and certainly Dot Records was one of the biggest labels in terms of doing that," explained Cary E. Mansfield, Varese Vintage's Director of Catalog A&R. "A lot of the black hits are now being played on the radio, and unfortunately that means the Dot versions are in danger of being forgotten. The 'Music of Your Life' format radio stations still play these songs, though; in fact, I talked to a lot of those stations and they were grateful to get these CD's because the music hasn't been available for years."

Disregarding the contributions of Dot Records would be a tragic mistake. Throughout its nearly 25-year history, Dot was home to talent ranging from word-jazzer Ken Nordine (a younger generation may remember his dulcet tones on Levi's commercials) all the way to Leonard Nimoy and William Shatner (yes, *that* Leonard Nimoy and William Shatner). What did Wink Martindale do before capping his teeth for a game show host career? Why, he recorded "Deck of Cards" for Dot.

Though a multifaceted shop — Dot was last known as home to many country artists (Donna Fargo, Barbara Mandrell, Joe Stampley) — the Varese Vintage CD's concentrate on the mid- to late-'50s manifestation of the label. At that time, nary a move was made without the direct involvement of Dot's founder, Randy Wood.

ABOVE: Where it all started. Photo courtesy of Don McGuire.

Randy's Record Shop, Gallatin, Tennessee, was the headquarters for Dot Records, which recorded and represented the Hilltoppers for so many years. (Sacca Collection.)

Whitey Sanders's tribute to the Hilltoppers, his classmates at Western. *Toast of the Town,* October 26, 1952. (WKU archives.)

7 Latter-Day Hilltoppers

The original Hilltoppers (Billy, Jimmy, Don, Seymour) may have gone their separate ways by 1963, but one place always remained common ground: Kentucky, particularly Bowling Green and the campus of Western. Each came back at every opportunity. This was, after all, where their short but fabulous career had started, and south central Kentucky was home to them in more ways than one.

Billy Vaughn, for example, returned to his hometown, Glasgow, in 1965 (there had already been a Billy Vaughn Day in Glasgow in July 1962) to participate in the celebration of a promotional movie, *Wonders of Kentucky,* for which he had been asked to write the score. He said that he almost turned down the offer: "I was afraid I couldn't do justice to it." Some of his friends, however, were "persuasive." Mack Sisk, a former Western student and editor of the *College Heights Herald,* knew Vaughn personally and approached him about the project. Billy not only agreed to write the score: he said he would do it gratis and pay his own way from California to Kentucky to attend the premiere.[1]

Noted *Courier-Journal* columnist Joe Creason wrote the commentary, and movie star Tom Ewell, from Owensboro, did the narration. S. Rayburn Watkins of Louisville was appointed by Governor Ned Breathitt as the chair of the Wonders of Kentucky Committee. When Watkins and his group described the project to Billy Vaughn, "he went far beyond anything we might have asked. He not only donated the professional services of his wonderful big band but also worked with some of his musically inventive people to produce six or seven original songs for the film, tied nicely to the script." The film was produced by Foster Films of New York. Columbia Pictures picked up *The Wonders of Kentucky,* which ultimately reached some six thousand theatres throughout the United States, and audiences of more than 200 million people throughout the world. (It played first in Bowling Green at Lost River and Riverside drive-ins, and at the Capital Theater.)[2]

For Vaughn, the job posed no problems. "I was writing about a State that gets more beautiful all the time," he said. His lyrics extol the virtues of a Kentucky vacation and a sunset on the Ohio River as it flows through Louisville. "Off to the Races" celebrates the wonder and excitement of the Kentucky Derby. Vaughn was nominated for an Academy Award in 1965 for his song "Louisville—My Home Town," which was played in the documentary. He later told a reporter that of all his musical arrangements and hits, he was "most proud" of the Academy Award nomination for the music in *Wonders of Kentucky.*[3]

He went home to Glasgow to visit kinfolk during the time he was in Kentucky for the premiere of *Wonders of Kentucky.* "He's the same old Billy," his mother, Sally, admiringly said. "Success hasn't changed him one bit." Billy sat out in the front yard at the Glasgow home of his sister, Coogie. Cars drove by, and many of their occupants recognized Billy and stopped to say hello. Billy returned the greetings. "Here, I'm Billy. Not a man who makes records in California. Just Billy," he told a reporter.[4]

In the downtown areas of cities like Louisville and Glasgow, however, sometimes people did not recognize Billy Vaughn's name, at least without prompting. At such times, he was always described first as a "singing Hilltopper." (One does not use the phrase "singing Hilltopper" with the past tense. Once a singing Hilltopper, always a singing Hilltopper.) Second, his fellow Kentuckians brought up the very successful Billy Vaughn Orchestra, which, during the past six or so years, had presented one notable song after another to the American public. Billy never got upset (it would have been uncharacteristic if he had) when people in his home state did not recognize him. "There is really no reason for you to know me," he frequently told puzzled fans, "but you've heard my music." Yes, indeed, they had, and after a few titles, the fans recognized him. There seemed to be so much love and affection between Billy Vaughn and his Kentucky fans and compatriots that, as time passed by, he thought more and more about returning home to his native state. He did just that in 1977, moving to Bowling Green and beginning a new phase of his life and career. He bought a home in Bowling Green, "a little lean-to," for which he paid $39,000.[5]

In 1969 Billy and his band started traveling to Japan every November. They became so popular that he continued these trips until the late eighties. In fact, over time he became more popular in Japan than in the United States, though his instrumental recordings in the United States outnumbered those of any other musician. He and his Billy Vaughn Singers discovered Japanese country-western singing star Eddy Fukano. "The Japanese are very giving people," Billy told columnist Herman

Lowe. "They especially like the Christmas season." He was, however, "shy" at the microphone. He always got a native Japanese to do the emceeing for his shows. The only area where Billy Vaughn was "not shy" was when he was writing music. He also became popular in South Africa, all the countries of South America, Germany, and many oriental countries besides Japan. Everywhere Billy traveled, at one point or another in his programs, he told his audiences that he was one of the original singing Hilltoppers. His music remained "simple" (not "simplistic"), just like that of the Hilltoppers. "Most people don't want to have to strain and get intellectually involved to enjoy music," Billy liked to say. He even kept up his "southern drawl" and always said "ma'am," and "sir" to the women and men he met. He personified not only the southern gentleman but also the very best of the Hilltopper tradition itself.[6]

His musical arrangements were primarily in the style of Glenn Miller or Tommy Dorsey. He did not like Stan Kenton's musical arrangements because Kenton's eight to ten brasses drove out all the reeds. First and foremost in an orchestra, Billy Vaughn maintained, you have to have the reeds. Without the reeds, music becomes merely the "science of sound," with a scarcity of harmony.[7]

Billy was not the only one of the original Hilltoppers who seemed to be in constant movement, although Don and Seymour had apparently settled into their new careers quite well. Jimmy Sacca, in Jackson, Mississippi, tried to make a go of it with the National Educational Consultants, but he found that more and more he was involved in his restaurant-cum-nightclub, the Celebrity Lounge. As the name indicates, numerous local celebrities performed here, and sometimes Jimmy himself did. But the old "makeup," as Don McGuire had said years ago, wouldn't rub off. It was there for good.

Sacca gladly accepted an invitation to return to Lockport, New York, his hometown, to perform before an enthusiastic high school audience of some four hundred students, as well as at the "Vaudeville, '69" program sponsored by the local Lions Club. Backed up by Jacky Diehl's orchestra, Jimmy was thrilled to be accompanied in several songs by his old friends Eddie Crowe (now primarily a schoolteacher in the Lockport system) and Lou Mastor (who was performing mostly at nightclubs in Buffalo). A local reporter said that Jimmy Sacca's "voice [was] deeply resonant, and probably more mellow and mature now than when he was at the top." He was a "real trouper," still with that unique voice that set him apart from all the other groups.[8]

Such accolades influenced Jimmy Sacca to get back into the music business full-time. "I wanted to lead a normal life," he later admitted to a reporter, "but I found out that this, the road and music and all *is* my normal life." Therefore, he took his friend Jerry Mize's advice and formed a record label company of his own. The company was called 3 JJ, a name taken from the first initials of the three partners, Jimmy, Jerry, Jimmy. They went to an RCA recording studio in Nashville where Jimmy's old pal and fellow Hilltopper Karl Garvin supervised the sessions. The newly formed Hilltoppers cut four sides: "All These Things," "The World Outside," "The Hurt," and "I've Been There, Too." By 1968, the Hilltoppers recording group consisted of Jimmy Sacca; Karl Garvin; Jack Gruebel, who had been a part of Boots Randolph's performers; and Chuck Ayre, who previously had been with the Vagabonds. Unfortunately,

RCA's distribution capabilities were not up to Hilltopper standards, and their recordings did not sell well.[9]

Although he was mostly on the road in 1968 and 1969, Jimmy did manage to meet some important business people in Fort Walton Beach, Florida, who happened to own the local Holiday Inn. They convinced Jimmy that he and his group should come down from Jackson and perform, at least during the winter seasons, by offering him and his band the food and beverage concession at the inn. The band still had its piano (its trademark throughout the early years), but now added drums, played by Larry Boullion and sometimes by Jack Gruebel. Other talented musicians who worked with the latter-day Hilltoppers included Terry Cano at the keyboard, David Thompson on drums, Lou Mastor and Doug Cardoza (who had been with the old Hilltoppers) and Clive Dill (who also had been an earlier Hilltopper) on the vocals, the old singing stand-by, Karl Garvin, and, of course, Jimmy Sacca as the lead singer.[10]

The Holiday Inn in Fort Walton Beach became the new Hilltopper base around 1970. Newspaper and radio advertisements let the local residents know that the rejuvenated Hilltoppers were in town, and they turned out in droves. Of course, Florida is a tourist state, and when visitors from elsewhere read or heard these ads, they, too, flocked to the Holiday Inn.[11]

Unfortunately, the Fort Walton Holiday Inn was soon sold, and "in the renegotiation of their lease it was no longer advantageous" for the Hilltoppers to hold on to their concessions. They once again became a touring group, primarily performing in private nightclubs, rather than the larger venues of earlier days. In 1972, they toured throughout the United States and Europe without the press coverage that they had enjoyed just a few years before. It had to be demoralizing after the success of the previous tours in 1956 and 1958. On their 1972 tour, very few newspapers noticed their presence; they were performing for special interest groups rather than for a large variety of fans. But, as Jimmy may have thought, it was at least keeping the group together.[12]

They were definitely busy. Jimmy's son, Jimmy III, drove from Jackson, Mississippi, to Winter Haven, Florida, to spend a couple of weeks with his dad and the band. The group did an average of two shows and three dance sets each night in various places in central Florida. When Jimmy and Jimmy III visited Disney World, Jimmy always wanted to take a ride on the train or the boat, for those were among the few places where he could get any rest.[13]

There were many people in 1972 who, if they did not remember the Hilltoppers, certainly had parents who did. On November 2, 1972, at the forty-third WKU homecoming, the Hilltopper football team faced off against Middle Tennessee at L. T. Smith Stadium, losing a cliffhanger by the score of 21–17. The homecoming theme was "A Melody Gone By: Those Were the Days." The song "Those Were the Days," was produced by Paul McCartney of the Beatles and released on the Beatles' label, Apple. Based on a Russian melody by Boris Foman, "Dorogoi dlinnoya," the song, with words by poet Konstantin Podrevskii, was first popularized by Gene Raskin of the Limelighters. The best-known recording was the 1968 release by Mary Hopkin, which became extremely popular throughout the country. Its theme of reminiscence of youthful and romantic idealism fit the mood perfectly on that homecoming day for both the Hilltoppers and their audience.[14]

Billy Vaughn and his orchestra performed "Those Were the Days" and other popular tunes for the annual alumni dinner at the Garret Center on the Western campus. Vaughn announced to his delighted audience that his band and the original Hilltoppers would make several special appearances throughout homecoming weekend. And indeed they did. Billy, Jimmy, Don, and Seymour rode in the homecoming parade that started at ten that Saturday morning and happily waved to the crowds lining the streets of Bowling Green. They were scheduled to participate in pregame ceremonies to crown Alice Denise Gatewood, the university's first African American homecoming queen. The singers attended a postgame reception in E. A. Diddle Arena for "friends of Western," helping, of course, to increase monetary contributions to the university. At one point in the observances, Jimmy presented a gold record replica of "P.S. I Love You" to Western Kentucky University president Dero Downing.[15]

The really big event was the Hilltoppers' performance at halftime before an exuberant and appreciative audience of about nineteen thousand. It had been twenty years since the four had sung together on the Western campus. When the Hilltoppers had been in their ascendancy, most of those in attendance "were shaking their rattlers and rolling baby carriages." A *Courier-Journal* staff writer, Larry Wilkerson, described the scene:

> The four men who stood on the football field bore slight resemblance to the picture of the Hilltoppers of 1952 that hangs in a snack bar near campus.
>
> They were mature, graying, not flashing that Joe

College smile and sporting beanies and sweaters with a "W" on them.

The crowd loved them.

Jimmy Sacca still had the distinct mellow voice with "hanging" vowels at the end of each bar of music: this was his "open air" method that so many reporters and reviewers had remarked upon through the years. As he launched into the Hilltoppers' signature song, "Trying," his wife, Ann, remarked to a friend sitting with her in the stands, "Ouch, he still gives me goose pimples!"[16]

As the Hilltoppers' homecoming concert finale, they sang "P.S. I Love You." As a result, writer Wilkerson remarked, "those red towels that Westerners are famous for might have been used to daub at a few eyes, as many alumni were in the audience." Indeed, they were, and they and the Hilltoppers experienced a close, even loving, rapport with one another on this festive occasion, a homecoming to remember.[17]

A few weeks after the WKU homecoming, in February 1973, the Hilltoppers contracted with MGM Records for four songs: "Jamaica Farewell," "Little Things That You Do," "Sunshine and Love," and "One of a Kind." The instrumental sessions for these songs were done in Los Angeles, and the vocals were added in Memphis. Afterward, the whole package was returned to Los Angeles where MGM added two female voices. The Hilltoppers were thrilled to be recording again; they longed for the recognition of past years.[18]

Unfortunately, a number of things began to go wrong with these MGM recordings. First, singer Al Green also recorded "One of a Kind" for MGM, and MGM put the Hilltoppers' rendition on the shelf and never released it. "Jamaica Farewell" was offered to the public, but it was patterned "after the bass line of Johnny Nash's 'I Can See Clearly Now.'" So not even this effort was completely "Hilltopper," a fact that did not sit well with the group. Then, to make matters worse, an MGM public relations man, Jacques Amann, told them that there had recently been an "MGM management upheaval" and that MGM was "having some financial difficulties" and was "stretched a little thin" in the matter of new "ventures." The company would therefore have to make some hard "determinations" between the Hilltoppers' "Sunshine and Love," and Judd Strunk's "Daisy a Day." As a record industry insider reported, "It was basically the toss of a coin that decided which was going to get the management push." Much to the consternation of the Hilltoppers, "Daisy a Day" got it.[19]

The Hilltoppers were used to struggle; they had experienced it from the beginning, with the military draft and the rise of rock 'n' roll when they were largely out of the scene. Now they had to compete with newcomers. They were not quitters, however; Jimmy, for one, was determined that they would go on as long as they possibly could. They once again turned away from so much recording and spent the next few years performing in nightclubs and supper clubs, and for special functions throughout the country.

In July 1974, for example, the Hilltoppers performed at the Masiello Restaurant and Lounge in Willoughby, Ohio, a suburb of Cleveland. "Nostalgia has been very good to Jimmy Sacca and the Hilltoppers," a local reporter wrote. This "refreshing group" was made up of Jimmy Sacca singing the lead, with Karl Garvin, Chuck Ayres, and Terry Cano at the organ providing the background. Their most popular songs at Masiello were "You, You, You," "Paper Doll," "Bad Bad Leroy Brown," "Rhumba Samba," and numerous country-western songs that fulfilled the Hilltoppers' spoken invitation to all the patrons: "Dancing welcomed with open arms."[20]

By 1975 a nostalgia craze for the 1950s was sweeping the country, and it benefited the Hilltoppers. Jimmy and his colleagues were now middle-aged, and that is the audience to whom they appealed. In May 1975, they played at the Ramada Inn on Hurstbourne Lane in Louisville. *Courier-Journal* staffer Billy Reed was on hand to report the events. Jimmy Sacca came out on the stage with a microphone in his hand, smiling at the audience. He told the audience to "reach out and take us by the hand, and we're gonna take a walk down that path of nostalgia until we get to the 1950's." Then he began to croon the old favorites with which the Hilltoppers had been identified over the years: "P.S. I Love You," "My Treasure," and, of course, "Trying."[21]

During one of the breaks in the show, reporter Reed asked Jimmy why he continued to perform. Why did he "work the road" and "grind it out" night after night? As an answer, Jimmy looked over at a man and a woman a few tables away, both probably in their fifties, who had obviously been enjoying the concert. "The pleasure I get out of it now," Jimmy said, "is people like those guys over there. I was a part of their lives, you know." The Hilltoppers may have evoked nostalgia in their listeners, but it was also clear that the group had mellow thoughts about their own lives and careers.[22]

Sadly, it seemed increasingly clear that the Hilltoppers, both "old" and "new," were soon to come at least to the physical end of their fantastic, all-too-short journey through the American musical landscape. Chuck Ayre left the the "new" Hilltoppers group; he was followed shortly by Jack Gruebel. Americans during the mid-seventies experienced an oil shortage, and cars and trucks lined up sometimes for miles to get a few gallons of gasoline. This emergency affected all entertainment groups who traveled by bus, the Hilltoppers included. It became too expensive for the Hilltoppers to travel from one engagement to another. The mid-seventies were simply a bad time for entertainers on the road.

But, wherever they went and whatever they did, the original Hilltoppers never forgot where they came from or what they had done on the Western campus that ultimately propelled them to international fame. In 1978, Don McGuire was chosen as the Western Alumni Association president. His job, essentially, was to put the university's best foot forward and to visit would-be Western students throughout the state's high schools and entice them to the Hill. The only requirement for the job, according to assistant alumni affairs director Gary Ransdell, was that McGuire not be "officially" connected with the university. He was not, nor in fact had he ever been, "official"; he was a proud alumnus, who in return had also made his school proud of him. By all accounts, he performed his job well. A decade later, Don became a lobbyist for WKU at the general assembly in Frankfort, replacing the university attorney, Bill Biven, who had died in 1987. Don said of this appointment, "Western doesn't really like the term 'lobbyist,' so I am 'representing' the university." His job was to put issues of importance to WKU before the solons and, hopefully, keep educational dollars flowing to Bowling Green. "It also helps," he added, "that I'm just about an hour from Frankfort," as he lived in Lexington.[23]

The Hilltoppers survived in some form in various incarnations until the early 1980s. The reports differ as to the date of the group's demise. One says 1958, another 1963, and still another 1979. This last date is somewhat accurate, for that is the year Jimmy Sacca and his son, Jimmy III, formed the Delta Entertainment Corporation, an entity that books artistic acts and singers around the country, and the Hilltoppers were no longer performing. This talent agency, which is still going strong today in Lexington, represents many establishments that use entertainment groups. For twenty-eight years, with a large number of ups and downs, the Hilltoppers had been part of the American musical scene.[24]

The first of the original Hilltoppers to pass away was Seymour Spiegelman, who died in 1987, at fifty-six, from complications following open-heart surgery. Two funeral services, one Protestant and one Jewish, were held for Seymour in Islip Terrace, New York, where he had been working for the Peter Pan Recording Company. His old friend and fellow singer Don McGuire said of him: "He had a unique zest for living. He was never unhappy, he was the eternal optimist who couldn't stand negative people." McGuire said that Seymour was "one of God's rare men," with the "infectious trademark of eternal youth," who "creatively refused to let the little boy inside him go away." At the time of Seymour's death, a Spiegelman musical scholarship was established at WKU. Awards are made each year to a student who is either majoring or minoring in music.[25]

Billy Vaughn and his wife, Smitty, had come back to Bowling Green in 1977, wanting to be near his family in Glasgow. During the decade that he stayed in his native state, Billy, although in semiretirement, formed a Dixieland jazz band with Doc and Timmy Livingston, Bob Flowers, Kenny Smith, Paul Satterfield, and Jeff Jones; the group played several nights a month at the Golden Branding Iron on the 31-W bypass. (The Golden Branding Iron was owned by Bill and Ada Williams, former proprietors of the Boots and Saddle Club, where Billy had started out so many years before.) Billy once again became a fixture in south-central Kentucky society. He had a music room built onto his house where he displayed the famous "twin saxophones," which he played at the same time. He continued sporadically to take his band to Japan and Germany, but his activities here were few in comparison with previous days. In Kentucky and nearby states like Tennessee, Indiana, and Ohio, the Dixieland jazz band performed, mostly on weekends, at several supper clubs, high schools, and colleges. Billy bought a "super van," equipped with television. Driving back to Bowling Green in the early hours of the morning, the band would usually find a good breakfast place, where Billy always paid for the food. "We never saw a stingy bone in his body," a band member noted. Billy was invited to play some hymns on his alto saxophone, solo, for the congregation of his church on Bowling Green's Cave Mill Road. He confessed to Dave Livingston that "he'd never been that nervous in his life." He was not a confident performer, but no better writer or arranger could be found in the entire country.[26]

Though Billy was at home in Kentucky with many of his kinfolks, his and Smitty's children were back in California, and Billy began to miss his grandchildren. He wrote a song in honor of each of his granddaughters: "Come Along Sweet Christy," "Traci's Tracks," and "Kelli." Billy and Smitty decided they should be closer to their children and grandchildren, and in late 1987, they left Bowling Green to return to California, this time to Encino. Their departure was traumatic enough to the Bowling Green community for the local newspaper to editorialize about it. "We hate to see the Vaughns leave," the *Daily News* said simply, echoing the sentiments of thousands of local residents. Billy's friend Willard Thomas drove the couple to the Nashville airport for their flight, accompanied by several citizens of Bowling Green and Glasgow. "A few tears were shed, and they were off," recalled Thomas.[27]

Of all the people who have at one time or another called themselves singing Hilltoppers, Vaughn was undoubtedly the most politically and socially conservative. Even during his first residency in the Golden State, he complained about high property taxes. He wrote back home to Kentucky that "we property owners have to support perfectly strong healthy welfare recipients." He blamed President Franklin D. Roosevelt's "give away" programs, and believed that Governor Ronald Reagan had ended the "fraud" on a state level by making sure that welfare money "went only to the needy." During his second California sojourn, he continued to be a strong supporter of Reagan, now in the White House, calling him the "father of the new democratic movement in Europe." He later defended Vice President Dan Quayle, whom the media "hated" only because he was a "strong conservative."[28]

While he may have given his views on politics and society to friends in letters, Vaughn avoided public statements, sticking, even after the onset of ill health, to his music-arranging and orchestra-conducting duties. He arranged "Sonny Gets the Blues," "Rainy Day," and "Yesterdays," for his own big band, and performed these and other songs several times at Disneyland, which "he loved," and at various clubs in Catalina. Despite the big-time aura of southern California, Billy Vaughn still missed Kentucky. After Vaughn moved to California, the Dixieland jazz band that he had formed while living in Bowling Green was led by his old friend Doc Livingston. "The people around there [Bowling Green] don't know how lucky they are," he exclaimed in a letter to Livingston. He said that members of his band in California were "great musicians," but as far as "natural ability" was concerned, "that group in Bowling Green was unique." His homesickness, or whatever it was, led him to inquire about the coffee drinkers on the square in Glasgow, Kentucky. There were an awful lot of caffeine fiends there, of which he had once been one, and he wanted to know about his old friends.[29]

Many of his neighbors in Encino were fellow musicians, with whom he formed an enclave of like-minded individuals. Possibly his best-known neighbor was Lawrence Welk, who in private came in for a lot of criticisms from his own musicians. Apparently, Welk in person was not as friendly and bubbly as on television. Billy Vaughn said, "Never once did I ask [Welk's musicians] what kind of a guy is he." They just volunteered the information. Many of them were stars because of Welk. "I like Welk but he doesn't remember me—nor does he remember most of his musicians." It could very well have been Welk's memory failures, often mistaken for indifference, that caused his unpopularity with some of his players.[30]

On March 21, 1988, Vaughn wrote gloomily to Livingston,

"We've been here [in California] for five months . . . and I've been sick just about all that time." He took strong medicines to keep lupus in remission and then came down with cataracts in both eyes. Only a little more than three years after returning to California, Billy fell ill with cancer and died in late September 1991. The *Lexington Herald-Leader* headlined its article about Vaughn's passing, "P.S. We'll Miss You, Hilltopper." The *Bowling Green Daily News* wrote that "Vaughn cast a magical spell through his music."[31]

Don McGuire said, "I remember Billy as the man who changed my life more than any human being on earth." He attended Billy's funeral and said in eulogy that Billy's talent was "like a tidal wave in the music world." Here was a man who could play at least nine different musical instruments and had never taken a music lesson in his life. Although Billy was shy, Don said, "he was the most talented mortal I've ever known."[32]

Another of Billy's close friends, Doc Livingston, noted that Billy Vaughn was a "small-town boy" who "put Glasgow on the map." No matter his accomplishments, Billy always remained humble and reachable. On the occasion of Billy Vaughn's death, Kelly Thompson publicly admitted what had long been suspected, that it had been he who let the four young men into Van Meter Auditorium for their first recording of "Trying" forty years before. In 1999, the Billy Vaughn scholarship was established at Western. The first recipient was Kirsten Gravely, a senior music major from Billy's hometown, Glasgow.[33]

Although the two surviving Hilltoppers, Jimmy Sacca and Don McGuire, were retired, in the 1990s and beyond, they were still active in their respective communities of Jackson,

Mississippi, and Lexington, Kentucky. Jimmy spent a great deal of time running the Celebrity Lounge, becoming well-known throughout the city and the state. In 1994 the Jackson Music Award Committee honored Sacca with a Jackie award for his contributions to music and the recording industry. The next year, his accomplishments were once again recognized, this time by the Mississippi legislature. Calling Sacca a "velvet-voiced baritone," the lawmakers recognized him for having been a part of the Hilltoppers, a group which in 1953 had been named number one in the country by the Jukebox Operators of America.[34]

In 1995 Bob Edwards of National Public Radio featured a story about the Hilltoppers and interviewed Don McGuire, who described the "chemistry" of the group. He said that Billy Vaughn arranged Hilltopper songs in a high "triad" harmony. McGuire remarked: "He [Billy Vaughn] knew that the simpler you make a song, the better chance . . . people had of hearing and understanding." Asked about favorite memories, Don was quick to mention singing "Till Then," which was popular with college kids in concerts. When the introduction to "Till Then" started and the Hilltoppers walked toward the microphones, "the kids recognized what was coming up, and I saw a guy reach and get his girlfriend's hand. It made the group feel good. It really did." He believed that, among other things, the Hilltoppers left a legacy among many music-loving couples who chose a favorite Hilltopper song as "our song."[35]

Psychologists tell us, says music scholar Michael Feinstein, that "a song appearing in our brain at any given moment is a clue about what is really going on in the sub-conscious. . . . A song exists for every conceivable emotion and mood, every nuance of possible behavior." As you grow older, other scholars say, "a song or singer's voice may suddenly transport you back to a specific moment and place in your life, sometimes many decades earlier." Whether you are twenty or eighty, a song can "evoke personal memories, images," and even fantasies.[36]

In 1996, Jimmy and Don, along with Billy and Seymour posthumously, were inducted into Western's Hall of Distinguished Alumni. They joined such notables as nuclear scientist Thomas B. Cook Jr.; financier Patricia Garrison-Corbin; Charles Kleiderer, inventor of the variable time fuse; and Clem Haskins, the Minnesota basketball coach who was a star player for Western during his college career and for a time piloted the team before going to Minneapolis. "It gives me goose bumps," Sacca said, "that we were a part of the history of Bowling Green. Believe me, it was an honor."[37]

Don moved to Lexington and takes great pride in a special room of his home where he exhibits all the Hilltopper memorabilia. He calls this room "the Shrine." On one wall hangs a short article by *Lexington Herald-Leader* columnist Don Edwards: "In the early 1950s, there were four things that made you feel great to be a Kentuckian—Adolph Rupp's basketball team, Paul "Bear" Bryant's football team, Rosemary Clooney on the movie screen in *White Christmas,* and The Hilltoppers doo-wahing a slow-dance number while young couples fell in love with their heads on each other's shoulders." On another wall are the large advertising signs that came from their tour of England in 1958. Also on a wall is a framed copy of their first million seller, "P.S. I Love You," as well as a record collage of the Hilltoppers' ten most successful tunes.[38]

The two remaining singing Hilltoppers are in constant demand for interviews by newspaper and magazine writers. They are a natural for human-interest stories. And the Hilltoppers are increasingly a part of anniversary celebrations to commemorate Kentucky accomplishments. For example, in early January 2000, the Kentucky History Center in Frankfort, under the direction of curator Mike Thomas, sponsored an exhibit on the Hilltoppers and invited Don McGuire to the event. One of his first responses to the invitation was, "Is it dressy? I guess I'll have to wear a tie." He never thought he would be a "sort of living exhibit . . . but it's an honor and I'm proud to be there." Someone asked him if he was going to sing on this occasion. He replied, "Now I sing eight measures in church, and my voice starts to go."[39]

In attendance at this living history exhibition was Bobbie Ann Mason, the first president of the Hilltoppers national fan club. She read from her book *Clear Springs* , which contains a lengthy description of her association with the singing group. Ed McClanahan was also on hand to read excerpts from his book, *Famous People I Have Known.* He told the audience that he had been a Hilltopper fan since the 1950s. "Their songs said the things I couldn't seem to say to the girls I thought I was in love with."[40]

In 2003 the Integra Bank in Bowling Green sponsored an extensive Hilltopper exhibit, "P.S. I Love You," at the Kentucky Museum on the Western campus. Starting on May 11, 2002, the exhibit ran for thirty-two months, under the direction of the museum's Sue Lynn McDaniel. The exhibit included the reel-to-reel tape recorder that had been used so long ago in recording "Trying"; a beanie and a sweater; the 1953 Cashbox trophy; photos and literary collections from Bobbie Ann Mason; and videos of the Hilltopper appearances on the Ed Sullivan and Steve Allen shows. Jimmy Sacca came back to campus to celebrate and promote a new disc entitled "P.S. I Love You." Hundreds of fans and admirers from Bowling Green and south-central Kentucky signed the guest book on this gala occasion.

Here in the opening years of the twenty-first century the fabulous Hilltoppers are still very much alive in the hearts and minds of hundreds of thousands of fans around the world. Many radio stations throughout the land are reviving the "oldies," or, as they are sometimes called, "the evergreens," because these are songs that "defy aging," outlast all fashions, and become perfect for the waves of nostalgia that periodically sweep over us. One oldies radio station is in Central City, Kentucky; there's at least one each in Bowling Green and Lexington, and there are three in Louisville, to say nothing about stations in the rest of the country on which the Hilltoppers are regularly featured. Of course, it is difficult if not impossible to tell whether this is establishing a trend in today's musical offerings. One can only hope.[41]

In summary, what can be made of the Hilltoppers these days? How do they speak to us today?

First, it must be reasserted that Billy, Jimmy, Don, and Seymour turned the word "Hilltopper" into a term in year-round use. Unlike numerous athletic teams at Western, they were always "in season," playing and performing almost nightly to tens of thousands of admiring fans on jukeboxes and records and in live performances.

Second, they gave the world a kind of music that, as McGuire explained, "didn't abuse anyone's ears." Their music put listeners into good moods that they usually shared with a loved one. There was an instant rapport between the singing Hilltoppers and the people who listened to them.[42]

Their decline can be attributed not to the quality of their music but to exigencies of the day. The military draft decimated the Hilltoppers as a singing group. Sacca was inducted in 1953, a scant eleven months after the original quartet was formed. When he was discharged in 1955, Don and Seymour put on military uniforms. By 1957, when the original group reunited, the country's musical tastes had changed. It was now Elvis and rock 'n' roll.

And then, one must remember, these young men had been separated from their wives and children, not only during military service, but also through all those months on the road. By the late fifties they were family men, and they yearned for the simple pleasures of family life. In a way, these sentiments had something to do with the ultimate breaking up of the original Hilltoppers. Jimmy and Ann Sacca's son, Terry, probably spoke for all the other Hilltopper children when he said that when he hears his father on the radio, he is the first to say to anyone around him, "That's my father's song." More importantly, however, Terry prefers to say, "That is my father," not particularly because of his great musical abilities, but because he is such a "loving husband and dad."[43]

It is not beyond the realm of possibility that in the early twenty-first century musical tastes can change once again. Music is as subject as any other form of art to what sociologist David J. Hargreaves calls "cyclical vogues." Americans today seem to be in a conservative frame of mind, and this probably augurs well for the kind of sentiment that the Hilltoppers generated with their love ballads. "Family values" are important to millions of Americans today. Most assuredly, the Hilltoppers in their heyday exemplified the idea that the family is the basic unit of any civilized society, and it must be nurtured. Lose family and you've lost it all. "The American public today is crying out for nice music," said one of the Hilltoppers' longtime friends, Charles Black, of Morgantown, Kentucky. "They want rhythm and pretty sounds and harmony."[44]

Many modern television commercials offer for sale to eager purchasers classic rock 'n' roll, old-time rhythm and blues, historic blues, and even country and western honky-tonk songs. Videos of singing groups including the Four Lads, the Platters, the Four Freshmen, and the Hilltoppers are regularly featured. Under these circumstances there could very well be a Hilltopper revival, at least in the form of old jukebox favorites and recordings of their top tunes. In fact, this is already beginning to happen. In 1994 Varese Sarabande Records released a compact disc entitled *P.S. I Love You: The Best of the Hilltoppers,* featuring Jimmy Sacca. This CD highlighted twenty-one Hilltopper songs that had made the top forty list. The liner notes were written by Bobbie Ann Mason. Since then, *The Best of the Doo Wop Collection by the Hilltoppers* has appeared, with the group singing thirty of their best-known songs. This collection was put together by Rock and Roll Records, under license from a company in the Netherlands. Reader's Digest Music, among its TV appeals, has advertised "P.S. I Love You," Madacy Records has touted "Only You," and Sony has emphasized the Hilltoppers in its collection *Golden Groups of 1954.* There is no way that the Hilltoppers from Western Kentucky State College will ever disappear from the American musical scene.

They may have come from a small institution of higher

education in Bowling Green, Kentucky, but their fame was universal. Western Kentucky University has produced many individuals of whom it can be proud—nuclear scientists, astronauts, chemists, biologists, television pioneers, entrepreneurs, generals, poets, writers, novelists, essayists, academicians, and many more. Right at the top of the list have always been the singing Hilltoppers. They did Western Kentucky State College, later WKU, proud. As long as there are students on the Hill—and that will be for some time—the singing Hilltoppers will never be forgotten. Indeed, they will be treasured forever.

Acknowledgments

Many people helped me to research and write this book, and I am grateful to each and every one of them. At Western Kentucky University, history department chair Richard Weigel read the manuscript and made helpful improvements. Department secretary Marsha Skipworth helped in many ways with this project. Nancy Marshall of the Helm-Cravens Library was always on hand to look up difficult-to-find sources, and I am most appreciative of her help. My graduate assistants, Caleb Pickering, Jonathan Chilcote, Crystal McFarland, and Phillip Shaw, were unstinting in their efforts to put this work together. I deeply appreciate their help.

At the University Archives, Sue Lynn McDaniel was extremely efficient in getting materials to me and advising me on the details of the project. I cannot thank Sue Lynn enough, especially for compiling the discography. Others in the Kentucky Library and Museum who helped in many important ways are Nancy Baird, Reid Brigl, Earlene Chelf, Amanda Hardin, Pat Hodges, Jennifer Howard, Sarah McCaslin, Connie Mills, Lynn Niedermeier, Leonetta Strange, and Sally Ann Strickler. The Kentucky Library and Museum on the campus of Western Kentucky University is a place in which all Kentuckians can rightfully take pride. Josh Hawkins of the Western office of alumni relations and Sean Kinder of Helm-Cravens helped procure some much-needed materials. I thank both these young gentlemen for their help. If I have overlooked anyone here, please forgive me. My friend and colleague, Bill Shurck, from the Bowling Green State University in Ohio, read the entire manuscript and put his expertise at my disposal. I thank him very much. I also thank Cheryl Hoffman, of Hyattsville, Maryland, for her excellent copyediting of this manuscript.

I am grateful to Doc Livingston and Lee Robertson for writing such fine forewords to my work on the Hilltoppers. Bobbie Ann Mason allowed me access to her collection at Western, read the first three chapters of the manuscript, and made useful comments on them. Certainly, I extend my thanks to Don McGuire and Jimmy Sacca. They granted interviews and access to their collections, and at every stage of the research, they gave me their encouragement. Thank you.

To all those who wrote to me, either by e-mail or "snail" mail, and granted interviews, thank you very much indeed. I could not have written this book without you.

And last, but certainly not least, I wish once again to express my gratitude to my lovely family: my daughters, Beverly and Hilary; my sons, Daniel and Matthew; my granddaughters, Colleen, Megan, and Katharine; my grandsons, Travis, Patrick, Austin, Liam, Rowan, Carlton, David, and Finn. And to Steve and to Arthur and to Chris and to Ling and to Elaine and Alec and to Grace. And, as always, to Pat.

Annotated Discography

Compiled by Sue Lynn Stone McDaniel

Unless otherwise noted, Dot Records released the Hilltoppers' recordings that featured Jimmy Sacca as lead vocalist. Randy Wood produced the original recordings.

Dot Records' extended-play (EP) records have DEP as prefix to their catalog number; long-playing record albums' catalog numbers use DLP.

Song credits are given the first time a title appears.

1952

"Trying" / "You Made Up My Mind" (15018)

"Trying" by Billy Vaughn

First advertised in *Billboard*, May 24; first charted in *Billboard*, August 23; highest *Billboard* chart position, no. 7.

Billboard Honor Roll of Hits: Highest position, no. 9; 11 weeks (October 25, November 8–January 10, 1953).

Ranked no. 38 on *Billboard*'s "1952's Top Tunes" (*Billboard*, December 20)

"'Trying' sold over 750,000 copies and stayed on best seller lists for 23 consecutive weeks." (*Billboard*, October 9, 1954)

The Hilltoppers' first televised performance was on Ed Sullivan's *Toast of the Town*, CBS-TV, October 26. The song was also sung on *The Perry Como Show*, CBS-TV, November 14; and on *The Eddy Arnold Show*, ABC-TV, June 7, 1957.

Also recorded by J. Desmond (Coral 608231), Ella Fitzgerald (Decca 28375), R. Gordon (RPM 369), J. Palmer (Mercury 5904), and T. Rhodes (King 4556).

Released with flip side "D-A-R-L-I-N" in 1956 by London Records (HL 8298).

"You Made Up My Mind" by Billy Vaughn

"Must I Cry Again" / "I Keep Telling Myself" (15034)

"Must I Cry Again" by Lincoln Chase / Lloyd Pemberton / Jerry Valentine

Operator's Pick, January 10, 1953; first advertised in *Billboard*, January 17, 1953; highest *Billboard* chart position, no. 15.

Ranked by *Billboard* as no. 38 on its 1952 Top Tunes list and no. 29 on its 1952 Top Popular Records According to Retail Sales list.

"I Keep Telling Myself" by Billy Vaughn

1953

"If I Were King" / "I Can't Lie to Myself" (15055)

"If I Were King" by Billy Vaughn

Only territorial (not national) on *Billboard* charts.

"I Can't Lie to Myself" by Jimmy James / Bob Hart

First advertised (full page) in *Billboard*, February 28; second full-page ad, March 7.

"P.S. I Love You" / "I'd Rather Die Young (Than Grow Old without You)" (15085)

"P.S. I Love You" by Johnny Mercer / Gordon Jenkins

First advertised in *Billboard*, June 13; highest *Billboard* chart position, no. 4

Billboard Honor Roll of Hits: Highest position, no. 6; 7 weeks (August 1–29, September 19 and 26).

Billboard's review of the release described "P.S. I Love You" as "small talk in the form of a musical letter [that] makes listenable disk fare. Might win spins" (*Billboard*, May 9, 1953, p. 24.)

Ranked by *Billboard* as no. 18 on 1953's Top Tunes, no. 16 on 1953's Top Popular Records According to Retail Sales, no. 15 on 1953's Top Popular Records According to Disk Jockey Plays, and no. 19 on 1953's Top Popular Records According to Juke Box Plays.

The Hilltoppers sang the song on *The Patti Page Show*, NBC-TV, August 12; *The Sammy Kaye Show*, NBC-TV, September 5; and *The Kate Smith Hour*, NBC-TV, September 23. Jimmy Sacca, Seymour Spiegelman, Karl Garvin, and Eddie Crowe sang on *Milton Berle's Buick Hour*, NBC-TV, January 12, 1954. Jimmy Sacca, Don McGuire, Seymour Spiegelman, and Eddie Crowe sang on *Cross-Canada Hit Parade* CBC-TV, in March 1957; "Marianne" hit no. 1 in Canada. Jimmy Sacca, Don McGuire, Seymour Spiegelman, and Eddie Crowe sang on *The Eddy Arnold Show*, ABC-TV, June 7, 1957.

Presented with Gold Record for song sales over a million copies on *The Art Ford Show* in New York, March 5, 1954.

Also recorded by J. Bruno (Banner 512), C. Cavallaro (Decca 24955), Four Vagabonds (Apollo 1057), Gordon Jenkins (Decca 27171), C. Stapleton (London 282), and S. Stitt (Prestige 757).

"I'd Rather Die Young (Than Grow Old Without You)" by Beasley Smith / Billy Vaughn / Randy Wood

First advertised (two full pages) in *Billboard*, May 2; second full-page ad, June 6; highest *Billboard* chart position, no. 8.

Billboard Honor Roll of Hits: Highest position, no. 20; 7 weeks (June 20, July 4–18, August 15–29).

Sung on *The Patti Page Show*, NBC-TV, August 12.

"To Be Alone" / "Love Walked In" (15105) released September 26

"To Be Alone" by Billy Vaughn

First advertised (two full pages) in *Billboard*, September 26; second full-page ad notes 300,000 copies sold in three weeks, October 17; highest *Billboard* chart position, no. 8.

Billboard Honor Roll of Hits: Highest position, no. 14; 4 weeks (November 21–December 5).

Note: Monologue voiced by Don McGuire.

"Love Walked In" by George Gershwin / Ira Gershwin

First advertised in *Billboard*, November 21; highest *Billboard* chart position, no. 8.

Billboard Honor Roll of Hits: Highest position, no. 13; 5 weeks (October 31, November 14–December 5).

"The Hilltoppers belt out the old Gershwin standard with plenty of beat. It looks like another big one for the boys, and a coin-grabber." *Billboard* review, October 3.

Released by London Records (HL 8003) and in Canada by Quality Records (1157).

***The Hilltoppers* (DEP-1-1006)**

"You Made Up My Mind" / "Must I Cry Again" / "Trying" / "I Keep Telling Myself"

Advertised in *Billboard*, November 21, 1953; October 9, 1954.

Note: Some copies of the extended-play record label read DEP-112.

***The Hilltoppers Sing* (DEP-1-1007)**

"I Can't Lie to Myself" / "If I Were King" / "I'd Rather Die Young" / "P.S. I Love You"

"I Can't Lie to Myself" by Jimmy James / Bob Hart

Advertised in *Billboard*, November 21, 1953; October 9, 1954.

Note: Some copies of the extended-play record label read DEP-113.

***The Hilltoppers* (DEP-1-1008)**

"For Keeps" / "Bouquets And Kisses" / "I Found Your Letter"/ "Till Then"

"For Keeps," "Bouquets And Kisses" and "I Found Your Letter" by Billy Vaughn

"Till Then" by Guy Wood / Sol Marcus / Eddie Seiler

Advertised in *Billboard*, November 21, 1953; October 9, 1954. Ranked no. 45 on *Billboard*'s 1954 Top Tunes list.

Note: Cover reads DEP-1-1008; extended-play record label reads DEP-114.

The Hilltoppers (DEP-1-1009)

"Time Will Tell" / "There Is No Greater Love" / "Blue Eyes Crying in the Rain"/ "From the Vine Came the Grape"

"There Is No Greater Love" by Isham Jones / Marty Symes

"Blue Eyes Crying in the Rain" by Fred Rose

"From the Vine Came the Grape" by Paul Cunningham / Leonard Whitcup

Advertised in *Billboard*, November 21, 1953; October 9, 1954.

Note: Cover reads DEP-1-1009; extended-play record label reads DEP-115.

1954

The Hilltoppers (DLP-105)

"Till Then" / "For Keeps"/ "Time Will Tell"/ "I Found Your Letter"/ "Bouquets and Kisses" / "There Is No Greater Love" / "Blue Eyes Crying in the Rain"/ "From the Vine Came the Grape"

Advertised in *Billboard*, November 21, 1953; October 9, 1954.

Note: Dot extend-play records 1008 and 1009 combined.

"From the Vine Came the Grape" / "Time Will Tell" (15127)

"From the Vine Came the Grape"

First advertised (full page) in *Billboard*, January 9; second full-page ad, January 23; highest *Billboard* chart position, no. 8

Billboard Honor Roll of Hits: Highest position, no. 7; 12 weeks (February 13–May 1). Ranked no. 32 on *Billboard*'s 1954 Top Tunes list.

Sung on Dave Garroway NBC-TV show, May 21.

Also released by London Records (HL 8026) and on Tops in Pops also with songs by Gale Storm, the Fontane Sisters, and Billy Vaughn in Denmark as Dot (DEP-510).

Also recorded by the Gaylords on Mercury Records.

"Time Will Tell" by Buddy Black

"Alone" / "You're All That I Need" (15130)

"Alone" by Arthur Freed / Nacio Herb Brown

Solo by Jimmy Sacca

Also released by London Records (HL 9038).

"You're All That I Need" by Milton Berle

Solo by Jimmy Sacca

Sung on *Milton Berle's Buick Hour*, NBC-TV, January 12.

First advertised in *Billboard*, January 16.

"Till Then" / "I Found Your Letter" (15132)

"Till Then"

First advertised (full page) in *Billboard*, January 9; highest *Billboard* chart position, no. 10.

Billboard Honor Roll of Hits: Highest position, no. 11; 8 weeks (February 6–March 27).

Sung on *The Perry Como Show*, CBS-TV, March 5.

"Poor Butterfly" / "Wrapped Up in a Dream" (15156)

"Poor Butterfly" by John Golden / Raymond Hubbell

First advertised (two full pages) in *Billboard*, March 27; second full-page ad, April 3; highest *Billboard* chart position, no. 12.

Billboard Honor Roll of Hits: Highest position, no. 19; 4 weeks (May 1–22).

Also released by London Records (HL 8070).

"Wrapped Up in a Dream" by William Best / Irving Berman

"Alone with my Heart" / "Mansion on the Hill" (15163)

"Alone with my Heart" by Beasley Smith / Randy Wood

Solo by Jimmy Sacca

"Mansion on the Hill" by Hank Williams/ Fred Rose

Solo by Jimmy Sacca

First advertised (full page) in *Billboard*, May 15; second full-page ad for "Mansion on the Hill," May 29.

"Sweetheart (Will You Remember)" / "The Old Cabaret" (15201)

"Sweetheart (Will You Remember)" by Sigmund Romberg / Rida J. Young

First advertised (full page) with list of six hits in *Billboard*, June 12.

Positive reports from St. Louis, Pittsburgh, Cincinnati, Providence, Cleveland, Nashville, Milwaukee, and Atlanta, *Billboard*, June 19, 1954, p. 30.

Released as "Will You Remember" by London Records (HL 8081).

"The Old Cabaret" by Beasley Smith / Billy Vaughn

Released by London Records (HL 8081) using the titles "Will You Remember" and "The Old Cabaret."

"At Sundown" / "Stormy Night" (15218)

"At Sundown" by Walter Donaldson

"Stormy Night" by Beasley Smith / Randy Wood

"If I Didn't Care" / "Bettina" (15220)

"If I Didn't Care" by Jack Lawrence

First advertised in *Billboard*, July 31; highest *Billboard* chart position, no. 17.

Released by London Records (HL 8092) and in Canada by Quality Records (1282).

"Bettina" by Paul Cunningham/ Eddy Rogers / Leonard Whitcup

"Time Waits for No One" / "You Try Somebody Else" (15249)

"Time Waits for No One" by Charles Tobias / Cliff Friend

First advertised in *Billboard*, October 9; full-page ad, October 16; highest *Billboard* chart position, no. 25.

Also released by London Records (HL 8116).

"You Try Somebody Else" by B. G. DeSylva / Lew Brown

"D-A-R-L-I-N" / "Frivolette" (15318)

"D-A-R-L-I-N" by James Cassin / Duke Enston / Teddy Powers

Advertised in *Billboard*, October 9; full-page ad, January 1, 1955.

Released with flip side "Trying" by London Records (HL 8298).

"Frivolette" by Edwin D. McMullen / Louis James / Edward Shelly

***The Hilltoppers Sing* (DEP-1-1011)**

"Glad, Glad, Glad" / "My Ann" / "Stormy Night" / "About a Quarter to Nine"

"Glad, Glad, Glad" by Billy Vaughn

"My Ann" by Jimmy Sacca

"About a Quarter to Nine" by Harry Warren / Al Dubin

Advertised as "new album" in *Billboard*, October 9.

***The Hilltoppers* (DEP-1-1012)**

"Frivolette" / "Tormented"/ "Without You" / "Can't We Try Again"

"Tormented" by Will Hudson

"Without You" by Asro / Hatrok

Advertised as "new album" in *Billboard*, October 9.

***The Hilltoppers* (DLP-106)**

"Glad, Glad, Glad" / "My Ann" / "Stormy Night" / "About a

Quarter to Nine" / "Frivolette"/ "Tormented" / "Without You" / "Can't We Try Again"

Advertised as "new album" in *Billboard* on October 9.

Billboard's "Review of New Popular Albums" on November 13 began, "The Hilltoppers have been the most consistent record sellers in the country for the past two years."

Note: Dot EPs 1011 and 1012 combined. Released in Canada by Quality Records (V-40).

1955

"The Door Is Still Open" / "Teardrops from My Eyes" (15351)

"The Door Is Still Open" by Chuck Willis

Full-page ad in *Billboard*, March 26.

Also recorded by the Cardinals.

"Teardrops from My Eyes" by Rudolph Toombs

Note: Dot label for 15351 reads "Tears Drops from My Eyes"

"The Kentuckian Song" / "I Must Be Dreaming" (15375)

"The Kentuckian Song" by Irving Gordon

First advertised in *Billboard*, June 11; highest *Billboard* chart position, no. 20.

Billboard Honor Roll of Hits: Highest position, no. 24; 9 weeks (July 23–30, August 13–20, September 3–October 1).

From the motion picture *The Kentuckian*, starring Burt Lancaster and produced by Hecht-Lancaster.

Also released by London Records (HLD 8168) and recorded by Eddy Arnold (Victor 20-6139), B. Benton (Okeh

7058), B. Bregman (Era 1002), J. Brown (MGM 12011), Guy Cherney (Mercury 70637), Bobby Sherwood (Coral 61439), P. Weston (Columbia 40527), and M. Wiseman (Dot 1262).

"I Must Be Dreamin'" by Jerry Leiber / Mike Stoller

"Searching" / "All I Need Is You" (15415)

"Searching" by Billy Vaughn / Randy Wood

First advertised (full page) in *Billboard*, September 10; highest *Billboard* chart position, no. 81.

Also released by London Records (HL 8208).

"All I Need Is You" by Freddy James / Doug Deane

"Only You" / "Until the Real Thing Comes Along" (15423)

"Only You" by Buck Ram

First advertised (full page) in *Billboard*, October 15; highest *Billboard* chart position, no. 8.

Billboard Honor Roll of Hits: Highest position, no. 6; 23 weeks (October 1, 1955–March 3, 1956).

"Only You" (London Records, HL 8221) charted on "Best Selling Pop Records in Britain" for 22 weeks, reaching no. 3 on the week ending May 5, 1956. During their 8-week 1956 tour, the Hilltoppers appeared on the British television shows *On the Town* (July 6) and *The Jack Jackson Show* (July 8).

Ranked no. 37 on *Billboard*'s 1954 Top Tunes list, with Platters and Hilltoppers having best-selling records.

Also performed by Louis Armstrong, Annie Ross, Steve Martin, the Platters, the Canadians, the Gremlins, Malcolm Vaughan, and Victor Silvester.

Note: Sheet music with Hilltoppers photograph is dated 1954.

"Until the Real Thing Comes Along" by Sammy Cohn / Saul Chaplin / L. E. Freeman / Mann Holiner / Alberta Nichols

"My Treasure" / "The Last Word in Love" (15437)

"My Treasure" by William Templeton / Cy Coben

First advertised (full page) in *Billboard*, December 10; highest *Billboard* chart position, no. 31.

Connie Francis originally recorded "My Treasure."

"The Last Word in Love" by Billy Vaughn

Also released by London Records (HL 8255).

The Hilltoppers Present Tops in Pops (DLP-3003)

Side 1: (1) "Trying" (2) "P.S. I Love You" (3) "I'd Rather Die Young" (4) "To Be Alone" (5) "Love Walked In" (6) "From the Vine Came the Grape"

Side 2: (1) "Till Then" (2) "The Kentuckian Song" (3) "If I Didn't Care" (4) "Tie Waits for No One" (5) "D-A-R-L-I-N" (6) "The Door Is Still Open"

First advertised in *Billboard* as part of larger ad with no image, March 31; ad on September 15 used photo of Hilltoppers Jimmy Sacca, Bob Gaye, Clive Dill, and Eddie Crowe.

Ultra high fidelity, monophonic.

Note: First cover art of girl drawn by Billy Vaughn; second cover with Western Kentucky State College beanies and pennant first advertised in *Billboard*, October 28.

Presenting the Hilltoppers (London REP 1012)

"Love Walked In" / "Poor Butterfly" / "Wrapped Up in a Dream" / "If I Didn't Care"

1956

"Do the Bop" / "When You're Alone" (15451)

"Do the Bop" by Billy Vaughn

Also released by London Records (HL 8255).

First advertised as "Their First Rocker" in *Billboard*, March 10, 1956.

"When You're Alone" by Marion Smith / Eleanor Broadwater

"So Tired" / "Faded Rose" (15459)

"So Tired" by Arthur L. Sizemore / George A. Little

"Faded Rose" by Billy Vaughn

First advertised using original Hilltoppers publicity photo in *Billboard*, April 14.

Also released by London Records (HL 8333).

"Eyes of Fire, Lips of Wine" / "I'm Walking through Heaven" (15468)

"Eyes of Fire, Lips of Wine" by Rafael René / Leon René

First advertised in *Billboard*, May 19; song titles flip in ads and there was never a full-page ad.

Sung on *The Eddy Arnold Show*, ABC, June 7.

"I'm Walking through Heaven" by Jimmie Lunceford / Joe Turner

Released by Dot Records in Sweden using catalog number D-45-1005.

"Ka-Ding-Dong" featuring Chuck Schroeder / "Into Each Life Some Rain Must Fall" featuring Jimmy Sacca (15489)

"Ka-Ding-Dong" by Ronnie Jordan / J. McDermott

First advertised with photo of Hilltoppers Jimmy Sacca, Bob Gaye, Clive Dill, and Eddie Crowe in *Billboard*, August 18; never a full-page ad; highest *Billboard* chart position, no. 38.

Billboard Honor Roll of Hits: Highest position, no. 21; 4 weeks (September 22–October 13).

Also recorded by the G-Clefs (Pilgrim 715) and the Diamonds.

"Into Each Life Some Rain Must Fall" by Allan Roberts / Doris Fisher

The Towering Hilltoppers (DLP-3029)

Side 1: (1) "I Can't Give You Anything but Love" (Jimmy McHugh / Dorothy Fields) (2) "Whispering Grass Don't Tell the Trees" (Doris Fisher / Fred Fisher) (3) "That Old Feeling" (Sammy Fain / Lew Brown) (4) "I Can't Get Started" (Vernon Duke / Ira Gershwin) (5) "The Gypsy" (Billy Reid) (6) "With Every Breath I Take" (Ralph Rainger / Leo Robin)

Side 2: (1) "At Sundown" (Walter Donaldson) (2) "Into Each Life Some Rain Must Fall" (Allan Roberts / Doris Fisher) (3) "Trouble in Mind" (Richard M. Jones) (4) "Why Baby" (Billy Vaughn / Beasley Smith) (5) "I'm Glad for Your Sake" (Jack Lawrence / Peter Tinturin) (6) "Maybe You'll Be There" (Rube Bloom / Sammy Gallop)

First advertised in *Billboard*, September 15.

Released by London Records' American Series as HA-D.2029 with additional songs "So Tired" as band 7 on side 1 and "Faded Rose" as band 7 on side 2.

"No Regrets" / "Until You're Mine" (15511)

"No Regrets" by Roy Ingraham / Harry Tobias

"Until You're Mine" by Ramona Redd

First advertised in full-page ad in *Billboard* on November 3 using photo of Hilltoppers Jimmy Sacca, Bob Gaye, Clive Dill, and Eddie Crowe.

Released in France by Versailles Records (45 S 539).

The Hilltoppers: Volume 2 (London, RE-D 1030)

"Blue Eyes Crying in the Rain" / "I Found Your Letter" / "Bouquets and Kisses" / "Till Then"

The Hilltoppers: Volume 3 (London, RE-D 1099)

"I'm Walking through Heaven with You" / "Eyes of Fire, Lips of Wine"/ "No Regrets"/ "Until You're Mine"

1957

"Marianne" / "You're Wasting Your Time (Tryin' to Lose the Blues)" (15537)

"Marianne" by Terry Gilkyson / Frank Miller / Richard Dehr

First advertised as "No. 1 Pop Version . . . The Hilltoppers Have It! with Billy Vaughn and His Orchestra" in *Billboard*, January 19; highest *Billboard* chart position, no. 3.

Jimmy Sacca, Karl Garvin, Lou Mastor, and Eddie Crowe sang on *The Steve Allen Show*, RCA-TV, February 24; Jimmy

Sacca, Don McGuire, Seymour Spiegelman, and Eddie Crowe sang on *Cross-Canada Hit Parade*, CBC-TV, in March; "Marianne" hit no. 1 in Canada that month.

Also recorded by Terry Gilkyson (Columbia 40817).

Also released by London Records (HLD 8381).

"You're Wasting Your Time (Tryin' to Lose the Blues)" by Billy Vaughn / Hy Heath

"I'm Serious" / "I Love My Girl" (15560)

"I'm Serious" by William E. Claunch / Quinton M. Cantrell

"I Love My Girl" by Robert P. Marcucci / Peter De Angelis

First advertised in *Billboard*, April 6.

Also released by London Records (HLD 8441) and in Denmark on *American Cocktail* with songs by Sanford Clark, Leroy Vandyke, and the Dell-Vikings (Dot DEP 513).

"A Fallen Star" / "Footsteps" (15594)

"A Fallen Star" by James Joiner

First advertised using contemporary image of Hilltoppers Jimmy Sacca, Seymour Spiegelman, Don McGuire, and Eddie Crowe in *Billboard*, June 10; photo of Hilltoppers Jimmy Sacca, Bob Gaye, Clive Dill, and Eddie Crowe in September 2 ad; highest *Billboard* chart position, no. 58, on August 28.

Billboard Honor Roll of Hits: Highest position no. 20; 6 weeks (July 15–August 19).

Also recorded by Jimmy Newman (Dot 15574) and by Ferlin Husky (Capitol F3742). Also released by London Records (HLD 8455).

BMI award-winning song.

"Footsteps" by Billy Vaughn

"Dedicated to You" / "My Cabin of Dreams" (15626)

"Dedicated to You" by Bruce B. Morgan / Egnoian

"My Cabin of Dreams" by Madison / Kenny / Frazzini

First advertised in *Billboard*, August 19.

"The Joker (That's What They Call Me)" / "Chicken Chicken" (15662)

"The Joker" by Billy Myles

First advertised using contemporary image of Jimmy Sacca, Seymour Spiegelman, Don McGuire, and Eddie Crowe in *Billboard*, October 21; highest *Billboard* chart position, no. 22.

Billboard Honor Roll of Hits: Highest position, no. 22; 6 weeks (December 2–January 6, 1958).

Released by London Records (HLD 8455) and in Australia by London Records as *London Hits* with songs sung by Pat Boone, Nick Todd, and Bonnie Guitar (EZA-1130).

Also recorded by Billy Myles.

"Chicken Chicken" by Vaughn / Tobias

Note: After the "original Hilltoppers" minus Billy Vaughn were reunited, Jimmy Sacca, Don McGuire, Eddie Crowe, and Seymour Spiegelman sang together again on this recording.

1958

***Love in Bloom* (DLP 3073)**

Side 1: (1) "Love in Bloom" (Leo Robin / Ralph Rainger)

(2) "I'm Confessin' (That I Love You)" (Don Neiburg / Al J. Dougherty / Ellis Reynolds) (3) "Then I'll Be Happy" (Sidney Clare / Lew Brown / Cliff Friend) (4) "Love (Your Spell Is Everywhere)" (Elsie Janis / Edmund Goulding) (5) "Our Love Is Here to Stay" (George Gershwin/ Ira Gershwin) (6) "This Love of Mine" (Frank Sinatra / Barry Parker / Henry W. Sanicola)

Side 2: (1) "Let's Fall in Love" (Harold Arlen / Ted Koehler) (2) "Together" (B. G. DeSylva / Lew Brown / Ray Henderson) (3) "So Beats My Heart for You" (F. D. Ballard / Charles E. Henderson / Tom L. Waring) (4) "(I Love You) For Sentimental Reasons" (Deek Watson / William H. Pat Best) (5) "Love Is Just around the Corner" (Leo Robin / Lewis E. Gensler) (6) "I Hadn't Anyone till You" (Ray Noble)

Arranged and conducted by Billy Vaughn. Jimmy Sacca, lead; Seymour Spiegelman, tenor; Eddie Crowe, baritone; Don McGuire, bass.

Ultra high fidelity.

No advertisements or mention in *Billboard*.

"Starry Eyes" / "You Sure Look Good to Me" (15712)

"Starry Eyes" by Moss / Cobb

"You Sure Look Good to Me" arranged by Billy Vaughn

First advertised using contemporary image of Jimmy Sacca, Seymour Spiegelman, Don McGuire, and Eddie Crowe in *Billboard*, March 3.

Released by London Records (HLD 8603).

"Peggy's Sister" / "Signorina" (15814)

"Peggy's Sister" by Billy Vaughn

"Signorina" by Crane / Jacobs

First advertised using contemporary image of Jimmy Sacca, Seymour Spiegelman, Don McGuire, and Eddie Crowe in *Billboard*, August 25

"Trying"/ "You're Nobody Till Somebody Loves You" (15857)

"You're Nobody Till Somebody Loves You" by Larry Stock / Russ Morgan / J. James Cavanaugh

"Trying" remake with orchestra conducted by Billy Vaughn ranked no. 93 in Top 100 in *Billboard*, May 12, and was included in the "Dot Parade of Best Sellers" advertisement, *Billboard*, May 26.

Reviewed November 10 and advertised November 17 in *Billboard*.

Note: Dot Records also released Billy Vaughn, "Tumbling Tumbleweeds" / "Trying" (15710) this year (full-page Dot ad in *Billboard*, March 10, 1958).

***The Hilltoppers Present Tops in Pops* (DLP-25003)**

"Electronically re-channeled for stereo."

First advertised in *Billboard*, May 4, 1959, as part of larger Dot Records ad.

Note: Same song titles in same order on DLP-3003.

1959

"I'd Rather Die Young" / "Welcome to My Heart" (15889)

"Welcome to My Heart" by Shirley Wolfe / Sy Soloway

Remake of "I'd Rather Die Young" recorded in England (*Hilltoppers Topics*, April 1, 1959, 1)

First advertised in *Billboard*, January 19.

"Lots of Luck" / "Lizzie Darlin'" (15958)

"Lots of Luck" by Jimmy Sacca; arranged and orchestra conducted by Billy Vaughn

"Lizzie Darlin'" by Beasley Smith; arranged and orchestra conducted by Billy Vaughn

First advertised in *Billboard* using photo of original Hilltoppers, June 22.

"Alone" / "The Prisoners Song" (16010)

"The Prisoners Song" by Guy Massey

"P.S. I Love You" / "Trying" (16022)

Billboard's Yesteryear Hits on March 24, 1958, ranked "P.S. I Love You" as no. 10.

"From the Vine Came the Grape" / "Love Walked In" (16024)

"Only You (and You Alone)" / "Till Then" (16025)

"Marianne" / "To Be Alone" (16039)

Released by London Records (HLD 8381)

1960

"P.S. I Love You" / "To Be Alone" (16054)

1963

"Only You" / "No Longer Lonely" (16556)

"No Longer Lonely" by Billy Vaughn

"P.S. I Love You" / "Trying" (112)

"From the Vine Came the Grape" / "Love Walked In" (113)

"Only You (and You Alone)" / "Till Then" (114)

"Only You (and You Alone)" by Buck Ram and Ande Rand

"Marianne" / "To Be Alone" (115)

"Only You" / "Until the Real Thing Comes Along" (London Records 45-HL-D.8221)

1967

"All These Things" / "The World Outside" (3J Records, 1000)

"All These Things" by Naomi Neville

"The World Outside" by John David Hurley / Ronnie Stephen Wilkins

Jimmy Sacca sang lead. Karl Garvin supervised the recording session with professional singers doing the background.

"The Hurt" / "I've Been There Too" (3J Records, 1007)

"The Hurt" by Jan Crutchfield

"I've Been There Too" by B. Rogers

Jimmy Sacca sang lead. Karl Garvin supervised the recording session with professional singers doing the background.

1973

"Jamaica Farewell" / "Sunshine and Love" (MGM Records, K14515)

"Jamaica Farewell" by Irving Burgess, arranged by Emory Gordy, produced by Harley Hatcher

"Sunshine and Love" by Mel Arakelian / Edward M. Beram, arranged by Emory Gordy, produced by Harley Hatcher

Jimmy Sacca, Karl Garvin, Jack Gruebel, and Chuck Ayre. MGM added two female voices after the February 1973 recording session.

"Little Things You Do" / "Sunshine and Love" (MGM Records, K14603)

"Little Things You Do" by J. W. Alexander, produced by Harley Hatcher

Jimmy Sacca, Karl Garvin, Jack Gruebel, and Chuck Ayre. MGM added two female voices after the February 1973 recording session.

1974

"P.S. I Love You" / "Trying" (ABC, P 2694)

"Only You" / "Till Then" (ABC, P 2715)

The Hilltoppers Sing Their Million Sellers (Souvenir Records, SLP100)

Song titles and order identical to *The Hilltoppers Present Tops in Pops* (DLP-3003).

Cover features a beach sunset. Although original recordings were used, the Hilltoppers' photograph on verso of cover is of the performing group composed of Chuck Ayre, Jack Gruebel, Karl Garvin, and Jimmy Sacca.

A later reissue, mastered by Randy Kling at Randy's Roost, includes "Only You" as band 7 of side 1 and "Marianne" as band 7 of side 2; the cover has a magnolia tree on the front and a photograph of the original Hilltoppers on the verso.

1990

The Hilltoppers Sing Their Million Sellers (Souvenir Records, SCS100)

Side 1: (1) "Trying" (2) "From the Vine Came the Grape" (3) "The Door Is Still Open" (4) "I'd Rather Die Young" (5) "D-A-R-L-I-N" (6) "If I Didn't Care" (7) "Only You"

Side 2: (1) "P.S. I Love You" (2) "Love Walked In" (3) "Till Then" (4) "The Kentuckian Song";(5) "Time Waits for No One" (6) "To Be Alone" (7) "Marianne"

Cassette tape produced by Jimmy Sacca.

1994

P.S. I Love You: The Best of the Hilltoppers (Varèse Vintage VSD-5524)

(1) "Trying" (2) "Must I Cry Again" (3) "I'd Rather Die Young" (4) "P.S. I Love You" (5) "To Be Alone" (6) "Love Walked In" (7) "From the Vine Came the Grape" (8) "Till Then" (9) "Poor Butterfly" (10) "D-A-R-L-I-N" (11) "If I Didn't Care" (12) "Time Waits for No One" (13) "The

Kentuckian Song" (14) "Only You (and You Alone)" (15) "My Treasure" (16) "Marianne" (17) "A Fallen Star" (18) "The Joker (That's What They Call Me)"

Compact disc digital recording manufactured by Varèse Sarbande Records, Inc., Studio City, California, and distributed by UNI Distribution Corporation, Universal City, California.

"This compilation ℗ 1994 MCA Records, Inc. released through the courtesy of MCA Records, Inc."

Notes by Bobbie Ann Mason. Numerous photographs courtesy of Bobbie Ann Mason, Don McGuire, and Jimmy Sacca.

"Dedicated to the memory of Billy Vaughn and Seymour Spiegelman."

2002

30 Rare Original Recordings: Best of Doo Wop Collection (Rock and Roll Records, HTGH-2002-30)

(1) "P.S. I Love You" (2) "Trying" (3) "Poor Butterfly" (4) "Time Waits for No One" (5) "Only You (and You Alone)" (6) "From the Vine Came the Grape" (7) "A Fallen Star" (8) "To Be Alone" (9) "Marianne" (10) "If I Didn't Care" (11) "The Kentuckian Song" (12) "Must I Cry Again" (13) "Till Then" (14) "My Treasure" (15) "I'd Rather Die Young" (16) "Love Walked In" (17) "D-A-R-L-I-N" (18) "The Joker (That's What They Call Me)"

2003

Golden Memories: The Ultimate Collection (SFI Records)

(1) "P.S. I Love You" (2) "Trying" (3) "Poor Butterfly" (4)

"Time Waits for No One" (5) "Only You (and You Alone)" (6) "From the Vine Came the Grape" (7) "A Fallen Star" (8) "To Be Alone" (9) "Marianne" (10) "If I Didn't Care" (11) "The Kentuckian Song" (12) "Must I Cry Again" (13) "Till Then" (14) "My Treasure" (15) "I'd Rather Die Young" (16) "Love Walked In" (17) "D-A-R-L-I-N" (18) "The Joker (That's What They Call Me)"

Sacca Family International Records compilation produced by Jimmy Sacca Jr. and James Sacca III, courtesy of MCA records under license from Universal Music Enterprises.

"Dedicated to the memory of Billy Vaughn, Seymour Spiegelman, Eddie Crowe, Karl Garvin, Al Bennett, James and Susan Sacca (Jimmy's Parents)."

2005

30 Greatest Hits! (Evergreen Records, 2691755)

(1) "Trying (2) "P.S. I Love You" (3) "A Fallen Tear [*sic*; should be *Star*]" (4) "Do the Bop" (5) "Till Then" (6) "I Must Be Dreaming" (7) "You Try Somebody Else" (8) "Ka-Ding-Dong" (9) "Time Waits for No One" (10) "I Love My Girl" (11) "Marianne" (12) "If I Didn't Care" (13) "From the Vine Came the Grape" (14) "Love Walked In" (15) "The Door Is Still Open" (16) "I'd Rather Die Young" (17) "The Joker" (18) "Until the Real Thing Comes Along" (19) "When You're Alone" (20) "The Kentuckian Song" (21) "No Regrets" (22) "So Tired" (23) "My Treasure" (24) "Poor Butterfly" (25) "Bettina" (26) "Teardrops in My Eyes" (27) "Must I Cry Again" (28) "The Last Word in Love" (29) "Only You (and You Alone)" (30) "To Be Alone"

Note: Based in Chicago, Evergreen Records converted many recordings to digital compact discs.

2006–2007

The Hilltoppers: Trying (Jasmine JASCD659)

A sixty-one-song compact disc of original recordings is due for release by Jasmine Records in late 2006 or early 2007.

Disc 1: (1) "Trying" (2) "You Made Up My Mind" (3) "Must I Cry Again" (4) "I Keep Telling Myself" (5) "If I Were King" (6) "I Can't Lie to Myself" (7) "I'd Rather Die Young (Than Grow Old without You)" (8) "P.S. I Love You" (9) "Love Walked In" (10) "To Be Alone" (11) "From the Vine Came the Grape" (12) "Time Will Tell" (13) "Till Then" (14) "I Found Your Letter" (15) "Poor Butterfly" (16) "Wrapped Up in a Dream" (17) "Sweetheart (Will You Remember)" (18) "The Old Cabaret" (19) "If I Didn't Care (20) "Bettina (21) "Time Waits for No One" (22) "You Try Somebody Else" (23) "Frivolette" (24) "The Door Is Still Open" (25) "The Kentuckian Song" (26) "I Must Be Dreaming" (27)"Searching" (28) "My Treasure"

Disc 2: (1) "Only You (and You Alone)" (2) "Until the Real Thing Comes Along" (3) "Ka-Ding-Dong" (4) "Into Each Life Some Rain Must Fall" (5) "Until You're Mine" (6) "Marianne" (7) "No Regrets" (8) "You're Wasting Your Time (Tryin' to Lose the Blues)" (9) "I'm Serious" (10) "I Love My Girl" (11) "A Fallen Star" (12) "Dedicated to You" (13) "The Joker (That's What They Call Me)" (14) "Can't We Try Again?" (15) "Do the Bop" (16) "My Cabin of Dreams" (17) "Chicken, Chicken" (18) "Faded Rose" (19) "D-A-R-L-I-N"

(20) "There Is No Greater Love" (21) "Blue Eyes Crying in the Rain" (22) "My Ann" (23) "Glad, Glad, Glad" (24) "Stormy Night" (25) "About a Quarter to Nine" (26) "Bouquets and Kisses" (27) "Without You" (28) "Tear Drops from My Eyes" (29) "Alone" (30) "You're All That I Need" (31) "Alone with My Heart" (32) "Mansion on the Hill"

Note: Jasmine Records is a UK reissue label specializing in music from the 1940s and 1950s, especially American artists.

Notes

Introduction

1. Stevie Wonder quoted in B. Lee Cooper, *Images of American Society in Popular Music: A Guide to Reflective Teaching* (Chicago: Nelson-Hall, 1982), xiv; Frith cited in Jonathan Epstein, *Adolescents and Their Music: If It's Too Loud, You're Too Old* (New York: Garland, 1994), xx; Theodor W. Adorno, *Introduction to the Sociology of Music* (New York: Seabury, 1976), 27, 33; Richard Aquila, *That Old Time Rock & Roll: A Chronicle of An Era, 1954–1963* (New York: Schirmer Books, 1989), 17.

2. Carlton Jackson, *J. I. Rodale: Apostle of Nonconformity* (New York: Pyramid Press, 1974), xiii; Alexis de Tocqueville, *Democracy in America,* ed. J. P. Mayer, 12th ed. (New York: Anchor Books, 1969), 209–10.

1. "Trying" Times

1. Sullivan quoted in Cori Bolger, "The Hilltoppers: 50s Boy Band Led by Jackson Man," *Jackson (Miss.) Clarion Ledger,* February 10, 2004.

2. Jason Riley, "From Barber to Music Wonder," *Bowling Green (Ky.) Daily News,* April 10, 1998.

3. Bobby McGuire, interview by author, March 17, 2004, Atlanta.

4. Sue Lynn Stone, "Voices from the Past," *Echo* (WKU), May/June, 2002, 15.

5. Greg Maddox, "A Little Touch of Magic," *Bowling Green Magazine,* Fall/Winter 1986, 26. See also Stone, "Voices from the Past."

6. *Weekly News* (England); April 11, 1956.

7. Don McGuire, interview by the author; April 28, 2004, Lexington, Ky.; Bolger, "The Hilltoppers."

8. Katherine Brown, "Kings of the Hill," *Kentucky Monthly,* December 1999, 16.

9. *Glasgow (Ky.) Daily Times,* October 16, 2000; C. Ray Hall, "Whatever Happened to …," *Louisville Courier-Journal,* May 27, 2000.

10. Dave Whitaker, "Hilltoppers Musical Variety, Are Invading New York to Appear on TV," *Park City (Bowling Green, Ky.) Daily News,* October 26, 1952.

11. Suzanne Higgason Waldrop, e-mail to the author, April 15, 2004; Lee Robertson, interview by the author, December 18, 2003, Bowling Green, Ky.; Whitaker, "Hilltoppers Musical Variety."

12. Charlotte "Coogie" Grissom, interview by the author, February 23, 2004, Glasgow, Ky.

13. Riley, "From Barber to Music Wonder."

14. Ace Dinning was the brother of Lou, Ginger, and Jeanne, the Dinning Sisters from Chicago. Their 1948 recording of "Buttons and Bows" hit the million-seller mark; Bill "the Greek" Ploumis, letter to Sue Lynn McDaniel, March 19, 2002, Kentucky Library, WKU; David "Doc" Livingston, interview by the author, January 11, 2004.

15. *Hilltopper Topics,* fanzine, Bobbie Ann Mason Collection, University Archives, Western Kentucky University (hereafter, Mason Collection).

16. Don McGuire, interview by the author, April 28, 2004, Lexington, Ky.; Warren Mahan, letter to the author, May 28, 2004; Lee Grace, "From the Hill to the Hit Parade," *College Heights Herald,* October 29, 1981.

17. Katherine Brown, "Kings of the Hill," *Kentucky Monthly,* December 1999, 16.

18. Cheryl Scott, "Begin the Beguine," *Western Alumni Magazine,* Winter, 1981, 5.

19. Joe Creason, "The Hilltoppers Quartet of Bowling Green Is on the Way to Becoming Musical Sensation," *Louisville Courier-Journal,* October 26, 1952.

20. McGuire interview.

21. Ploumis to McDaniel.

22. Nancy de Vincent, letter to the author, July 21, 2004.

23. DeVincent to author. Eighty-five-year-old DeVincent wrote: "All members of our group are gone. I'm the last leaf on the tree—just waiting for the heavenly breeze to carry me home."

24. Maddox, "Little Touch of Magic," 26.

25. Mike Callahan and David Edwards, "Randy Wood: The Dot Records Story," http://www.bsnpubs.com/dot/dotstory.html.

26. Brown, "Kings of the Hill," 16.

27. Jimmy Sacca, interview by the author, June 15, 2004, Lexington, Ky.; Brown, "Kings of the Hill," 16; Callahan and Edwards, "Randy Wood."

28. "Four Western Musicians Hit National Spotlight," *College Heights Herald,* June 27, 1952.

29. Creason, "Hilltoppers Quartet."

30. Creason, "Hilltoppers Quartet." See also Whitaker, "Hilltoppers Musical Variety."

31. Sacca, interview; Jim Warren, "An Original Boy Band—CD Celebrates Pop Music's Biggest Thing circa 1952: A Quartet of Guys from WKU," *Lexington Herald-Leader,* January 18, 2004.

32. Whitaker, "Hilltoppers Musical Variety."

33. Mahan to author; Sue Lynn McDaniel, e-mail to the author, September 2, 2004; Herman Lowe, "Billy Vaughn Began the Hilltopper Quartet at the Old Boots and Saddle," *Park City (Bowling Green, Ky.) Daily News,* November 19, 1987. In this same article, Lowe recounts a trip he and his wife, Em, made to Fort Lauderdale, Florida, during a Christmas season. The city was full of college students who were buying Hilltopper records. "When some of them found out we were from Bowling Green and knew The Hilltoppers, we immediately became somebody." One student learned that Lowe had sold the original Hilltopper sweaters, and "he wanted my autograph!"

34. Ploumis to McDaniel.

35. Brown, "Kings of the Hill," 17; H. B. Teeter, "Fly-Away Collegians," *Nashville Tennessean,* February 1, 1953.

36. Creason, "Hilltoppers Quartet."

2. A Gathering of The Hilltoppers

1. The most comprehensive history of Western Kentucky University to date is Lowell Harrison, *Western Kentucky University* (Lexington: University Press of Kentucky, 1987).

2. Irwin Spiegelman (Seymour's brother), e-mail to the author, August 10, 2004.

3. Jimmy Sacca, interview by the author, June 15, 2004; Lexington, Ky.

4. Sacca, interview.

5. Sacca, interview.

6. Sacca, interview.

7. Sacca, interview.

8. One must remember that the Crittenden Resolutions came from a Kentuckian in the immediate pre–Civil War period, resolutions that, if they had been adopted, might have prevented the conflict. Kentucky's most famous son, Henry Clay, often spoke about the state's unique position with respect to politics, economics, geography, and, especially, history.

9. The sales statistics for this million-record seller were generated by Dot Records. It was not until 1958 that the Recording Industry Association of America began certifying gold records; undated essay, Mason Collection.

10. Penelope Spiegelman Register, e-mail to the author, May 12, 2004; Suellyn Spiegelman Perry, e-mail to the author, April 7, 2005.

11. Brown, "Kings of the Hill."

12. Hilltopper Club of Great Britain, Slough, fanzine, December, 1956, Mason Collection.

13. John Rayner, "America's Top Vocal Groups," Hilltopper Club of Great Britain, Slough, fanzine, December, 1956, Mason Collection.

14. Jery Tillotson, e-mail to the author, July 14, 2004; anonymous, letter to Jimmy Sacca, August 16, 1992, Sacca Collection, Lexington, Ky.

15. Wayne Stierle, "The Hilltoppers: From Hit Pop to Vanishing Act," *Goldmine,* November 6, 1987, 24, 133.

16. The best treatment of cabaret laws is Paul Chevigny, *Gigs: Jazz and the Cabaret Laws in New York City* (New York: Routledge, 1991).

17. David J. Hargreaves, "Preference and Prejudice in Music: A Psychological Approach," *Popular Music and Society* 8, no. 2 (1982): 14; Larry Starr and Christopher Waterman, *American Popular Music: From Minstrelsy to MTV* (New York: Oxford University Press, 2003), 2.

18. Tillotson to author; Douglas "Smart Guy" (Melbourne, Australia), e-mail to the author, September 10, 2004.

19. Wayne Stierle, "The Fine Art of 'Covering' Hits," *Rock Magazine,* September 10, 1973, 42.

20. Bobby McGuire, interview by the author, March 17, 2004. Atlanta.

21. Simon Ward, column, *Daily Sketch* (London, England), July 11, 1956.

22. Pat Boone, telephone interview by the author, August 10, 2004.

23. Don J. Dampier, *Finding the Fifties* (Georgetown, Ky.: DJ Discovery Press, 2005), 58.

24. "The Popularity of Various Hilltopper Tunes According to a Survey Made by *Billboard* Magazine," Mason Collection; Sean McCollum, "Those Crazy Rockin' Teenagers," *New York Times,* February 23, 1957; Aquila, *That Old Time Rock & Roll*, 17; see also David Rowe, *Popular Cultures: Rock Music, Sport, and the Politics of Pleasure* (London: Sage, 1995), 9; Richard Peterson, "Why 1955? Explaining the Advent of Rock Music," *Popular Music,* January 1990, 98; Daniel Booth, "Who Do Youth Think They Are?" *Melody Maker,* May 15, 1999, 22; Starr and Waterman, *American Popular Music,* 195.

25. Don McGuire, interview by the author, April 28, 2004; Lexington, Ky.

26. Don McGuire, interview.

27. Irwin Spiegelman, e-mail.

28. Don McGuire, interview.

29. See "They're Really Teenagers at Heart: The Hilltoppers," *Recordland,* September 1954, 29.

30. Sacca, interview; Bennie Beach, interview by the author, January 6, 2004, Bowling Green, Ky.; "Four Western Musicians."

31. Warren Mahan, letter to the author, May 28, 2004.

32. Anonymous, interview by the author, February 7, 2004.

33. Mahan, letter.

34. Mahan, letter.

35. *Lexington Herald-Leader,* September 4, 1975; Ed McClanahan, *Famous People I Have Known* (New York: Farrar, Strauss, Giroux, 1985), 10; Sacca, interview.

36. Anonymous, interview by the author, January 24, 2005.

37. William Ploumis, e-mail to the author, November 21, 2003.

38. Ploumis, e-mail; Sacca, interview.

39. Sacca, interview.

40. William "Whitey" Sanders, e-mail to the author, March 20, 2005.

41. Bobbie Ann Mason, "Reaching the Stars: My Life as a Fifties Groupie," *New Yorker,* May 26, 1986.

42. *College Heights Herald,* December 11, 1953.

3. "Mixed-Up" Hilltoppers

1. *Hilltopper-ette: The Hilltopper Fan Club Magazine,* 1953.

2. *Hilltopper-ette,* 1953.

3. During the mid-fifties, the "concept of teenagers dancing to current hit songs was so anomalous that networks wanted no part of it." See John H. Jackson, *American Bandstand: Dick Clark and the Making of a Rock 'n' Roll Empire* (New York: Oxford University Press, 1997), x.

4. Bobby McGuire (Don's brother), interview by the author, March 17, 2004, Atlanta; Hall, "Whatever Happened to . . . ."

5. "Jimmy Sacca," *Lockport (N.Y.) Union Sun and Journal,* March 13, 1953; see also "The Hilltoppers Are Back," *Buffalo (N.Y.) Courier-Express,* February 27, 1953.

6. "Fans Fete Jimmy Sacca," *Lockport (N.Y.) Union Sun and Journal,* March 13, 1953.

7. Mason Collection, box 6, folder 27.

8. *Hilltopper Highlights,* August 1956.

9. *Meet the Hilltoppers,* pamphlet, Mason Collection.

10. *Meet the Hilltoppers.*

11. Bill Ladd, Almanac, *Louisville Courier-Journal,* December 26, 1953.

12. "Four Gunners Win Title," *Stars and Stripes,* Okinawa-Islands ed., August 26, 1954, Sacca Collection, Lexington; "Packed House Sees Rycom Finals of Barbershop Quartet Singing," *Ryukyuan Review,* August 22, 1954.

13. "Packed House Sees Rycom Finals."

14. *Hilltopper Fan Club Bulletin,* ed. 1, June 30, 1955, Mason Collection, folder 68.

15. Barry Bronson, "The Hilltoppers Offer Pure Nostalgia," *Lexington Herald-Leader,* September 6, 1975.

16. Maxine Caruthers to Bobbie Ann Mason, June 14, 1955, Mason Collection.

17. Remarks, Opening Ceremonies, Hilltopper Exhibit, Kentucky Building, May 11, 2002.

18. *Milton Berle Show,* January 12, 1954, NBC-TV.

19. Michael Kammen, *American Culture, American Tastes: Social Change and the Twentieth Century* (New York: Basic Books, 1999), 176; for additional information about the Frankfurt school and Theodor Adorno, the "sociologist of music," see Robert M. Crunden, *A Brief History of American Culture* (Armonk, N.Y.: M. E. Sharpe, 1996), 200–201.

20. *Hilltopper Highlights,* 1st ed., August 1956, Mason Collection.

21. Bobbie Ann Mason to Paul Garrett, February 22, 1953, Mason Collection, folder 73; Robert Cochran to Bobbie Ann Mason, March 4, 1953, Mason Collection, folder 73.

22. Bobbie Ann Mason to Western Alumni Office, May 20, 1954, Mason Collection, file 73; Cochran to Mason; Bobbie Ann Mason, e-mail to the author, March 6, 2005.

23. Kelly Thompson to Don McGuire, May 28, 1954, Mason Collection, folder 72.

24. Mason, "Reaching the Stars," 30.

25. Mason, "Reaching the Stars"; Pat Boone to Bobbie Ann Mason, July 18, 1955, Mason Collection.

26. Mason, "Reaching the Stars," 30; Bobbie Ann Mason, *Clear Springs: A Memoir* (New York: Random House, 1999), 102.

27. *Hilltopper Highlights,* no. 1, August 1956, University Archives, WKU.

28. *Hilltopper Highlights,* no. 1, August 1956.

29. Mason, "Reaching the Stars," 31.

30. Maxine Caruthers to Bobbie Ann Mason, May 27, 1955, Mason Collection, file 74.

31. Jimmy Sacca to Bobbie Ann Mason, June 2, 1955, Mason Collection, folder 72; Maxine Caruthers to Bobbie Ann Mason, June 29, 1955, Mason Collection, folder 74.

32. Mike Callahan and David Edwards, "The Dot Records Story, Part 3," http://www.bsnpubs.com/dot/dotstoryc.html. In 1967 Wood left Dot and formed a label, Ranwood, with Lawrence Welk. The next year, Gulf+Western bought Paramount; Dot was ultimately merged with ABC in 1974, primarily as a country label.

33. For a discussion of early rock 'n' roll, see James Miller, *Flowers in the Dustbin: The Rise of Rock and Roll* (New York: Simon & Schuster, 1999), 97–102; Starr and Waterman, *American Popular Music,* 2.

34. Jimmy Sacca to Bobbie Ann Mason, June 15, 1955, Mason Collection, folder 74.

35. *Ed Bonner Show,* KXOX, St. Louis, September 23, 1955, Mason Collection, folder 23; Penworthy composition book, Mason Collection.

36. Steve Schickel, *Inside Show Business,* October 29, 1955, WGN, Chicago; Mason Collection, folder 23, Penworthy composition book.

37. Caruthers to Mason, October 6, 1955; Sacca, interview.

38. *Hilltopper Topics,* March–April, 1956.

39. Mason, "Reaching the Stars," 33; *Mayfield (Ky.) Messenger,* January 13, 1956, Mason Collection, folder 65.

40. Mason, "Reaching the Stars"; *Mayfield (Ky.) Messenger,* January 13, 1956.

41. Mason, "Reaching the Stars"; *Mayfield (Ky.) Messenger,* January 13, 1956; Sacca, interview.

42. Mason, "Reaching the Stars," 33.

4. "Blimey, We've Gone Limey"

1. In fact, "Only You" stayed on British charts in 1956 for twenty-six weeks. Its popularity with English record buyers was instrumental in setting up the tour of the British Isles. Jimmy Sacca, curriculum vitae, Sacca Collection, Lexington.

2. June Harris, *What's On* (England), July 13, 1956.

3. *Hilltopper Topics,* January–February 1957. See also *Teenage Voice,* April 1957, and June 15–July 15, 1957, 7.

4. There are, of course, many explanations of why the English drive on the left side of the road. Probably the one that makes the most sense is that in the old days knights had to keep their sword hands free as they traveled along England's roads. Since most people are right-handed, this meant that the knights would have to ride on the left, so they could fend off any adversary that came their way. True? Who knows? But it's a good story. Also, the Hilltoppers learned that "limey" is actually a compliment. Since the English

were a seagoing people, spending many months at a time on the ocean, scurvy was a problem. To prevent this malady, English seamen loaded up with limes as much as they possibly could. Hence, the term "limey."

5. For example, here's some British English that most American students cannot understand. "The articulated lorry ran the shooting brake off onto the berm of the dual carriageway just before getting to the flyover. It damaged the bonnet considerably but did not touch the hood." (The semi eighteen-wheeler hit the station wagon and pushed it off to the shoulder of the four-lane highway just before they got to the bridge. The hood was damaged but not the top of the car.)

6. Tony Brown, "The Bane of Show Business," *Picturegoer,* August 11, 1956.

7. Doug Geddes, review of the Hilltoppers at Finsbury Park Empire, July 9, 1956, Hilltopper Club of Great Britain fanzine, Mason Collection; *Melody Maker,* July 14, 1956.

8. Geddes, review.

9. Geddes, review.

10. *Melody Maker,* July 14, 1956. Of course, the critic here did not name the songs the Hilltoppers performed. His review reflected the British analysts' propensity to be more "clever" than correct.

11. *The Stage,* July 12, 1956.

12. Donald Black, review of the Hilltoppers at Finsbury Park Empire, July 9, 1956, Hilltopper Club of Great Britain, fanzine, Mason Collection.

13. Black, review. See also "The Hilltoppers Come to Town," *Musical Express* (London), July 13, 1956; and *TV Mirror,* July 21, 1956.

14. Hilltopper Club of Great Britain fanzine, July 27, 1956, Mason Collection.

15. Hilltopper Club of Great Britain fanzine, July 27, 1956.

16. Simon Ward, column, *Daily Sketch,* July 11, 1956.

17. *Evening Citizen* (London), July 14, 1956.

18. Jay Warner, "The Hilltoppers," in *The Billboard Book of American Singing Groups: A History, 1940–1990* (New York: Billboard Books, 1992), 222; Carl Janusek and Nancy Janusek, "Interview with Jimmy Sacca and Chuck Ayres," *Discoveries,* May 1992, 8; *Hilltopper Highlights,* July 1956, on file in the Kentucky Building,

WKU Archives, Hilltopper Collection; C. Janusek and N. Janusek, "Interview with Sacca and Ayres," 8.

19. *Glasgow (Scotland) Evening News,* August 13, 1956; *Nottingham Guardian Journal,* August 29, 1956.

20. *Nottingham Guardian Journal,* August 29, 1956.

21. *Nottingham Guardian Journal,* August 29, 1956; *TV Mirror,* September 1, 1956.

22. What the English (and much of the rest of the world) call "football" is called "soccer" in the United States. *Daily Mail,* Manchester ed., September 13, 1956.

23. *Daily Mail,* Manchester ed., September 13, 1956; *Sheffield Star,* September 11, 1956.

24. *Sheffield Star,* September 11, 1956.

25. Major reviews were printed in *Manchester Evening Chronicle,* July 4, 1956; *Oldham Evening Chronicle,* July 5, 1956; *Stoke Newington Observer,* July 6, 1956; *Hornsley Journal,* July 6, 1956; *News Chronicle,* July 6, 1956; *Enfield Gazette,* July 6, 1956; *Evening Citizen* (London), July 11, 1956, and August 8 and 11, 1956; *Evening Telegraph and Post* (London), July 10, 1956; *Birmingham Evening Dispatch,* July 12, 1956; *The Stage,* July 12, 1956; *Birkenhead News,* July 28, 1956; *Liverpool Echo,* July 27, 1956; *Musical Express,* July 27, 1956; *Sunday Sun* (London), July 22, 1956; *Scottish Sunday Express,* August 5, 1956; *Lincolnshire Echo,* August 4, 1956; *Liverpool Evening Express,* July 31, 1956, and August 4, 1956; *Edinburgh Evening News,* August 7, 1956; *Glasgow Evening News,* August 13, 1956; *Glasgow Herald,* August 10, 1956; *Newcastle Journal,* August 16, 1956; and many others.

26. *Evening Dispatch* (London), August 7, 1956.

27. *Edinburgh Evening News,* August 7, 1956; *Liverpool Evening Express,* July 31, 1956.

28. *Evening News* (London), August 14, 1956; *Glasgow (Scotland) Herald,* August 14, 1956.

29. *Glasgow (Scotland) Herald,* August 14, 1956; *Daily Record and Mail,* August 24, 1956; *Yorkshire Post,* August 21, 1956; *TV Mirror,* September 15, 1956.

30. *Manchester Evening News,* August 28, 1956.

31. *The Stage,* July 12, 1956; *Lincolnshire Echo,* August 4, 1956; *Liverpool Evening Express,* August 4, 1956.

32. Jimmy Sacca, letter to *Hilltopper Topics,* January–February 1957.

33. Bobby Harrell, "Integration Celebrated: Diversity Sees 50th Year on Hill," *College Heights Herald,* February 14, 2006.

34. Hilltopper Club of Great Britain, bulletin 3, March 1957, Mason Collection, folder 27.

35. Hilltopper Club of Great Britain, bulletin 3; *Hilltopper Topics,* January–February, 1957.

36. *Hilltopper Topics,* January–February, 1957

37. *Hilltopper Topics,* January–February, 1957

38. *Steve Allen Show,* February 24, 1957, transcript, Sacca Collection.

39. *Steve Allen Show,* February 24, 1957.

40. *Steve Allen Show,* February 24, 1957.

41. "Hilltoppers Entertain at Casa Loma in St. Louis," *Hilltopper Topics,* March–April, 1957.

42. "Hail, the Gang's All Here!" *Hilltopper Topics,* March 20, 1957, Mason Collection, UA 94, box 6; Hilltopper Club of Great Britain, Bulletin 3.

43. Don McGuire, "Letter to Fans," *Hilltopper Topics,* January–February 1957, 3.

44. "Hilltoppers Star at Southern Illinois University Gathering," *Hilltopper Topics,* January–February 1957, 3.

45. *Hilltopper Topics,* May–June 1957; Carol Braddy, letter to the author; June 20, 2004.

46. Braddy to author.

47. Don McGuire, telephone conversation with the author, April 1, 2005.

48. Stierle, "Hilltoppers," 24. "Oldies" seemed to refer to the big bands of the World War II era. Particularly popular were Tommy Dorsey and Glenn Miller.

49. Stierle, "Hilltoppers," 24.

50. *Hilltopper Topics,* May–June 1957.

5. Hilltopper Tops

1. Hilltoppers Club of Great Britain, bulletin 3, March 1957, folder 27, Mason Collection.

2. *Billboard,* October 25, 1952, and November 1, 1952.

3. Peter Hesbacker, "Record World and Billboard Charts Compared: Single Hits, 1970–1979," *Popular Music and Society* 8, no. 2

(1982): 101; David Brackett, "The Politics and Practice of 'Crossover' in American Popular Music, 1963 to 1965," *Musical Quarterly* 78, no. 4 (Winter 1994): 775.

4. Barry A. Jeckell and Tamara Conniff, "It's a Musicians' Revolution," *USA Weekend,* February 24–26, 2006, 6; Simon Frith, *Music for Pleasure: Essays in the Sociology of Pop* (New York: Routledge, 1988), 106; Robert A. Stebbins, *The Barbershop Singer: Inside the Social World of a Musical Hobby* (Buffalo, N.Y.: University of Toronto Press, 1996), 3.

5. *Billboard,* December 20, 1952.

6. *Billboard,* February 28, 1953, and May 2, 1953.

7. Ann Sacca, letter to the author, May 3, 2005.

8. *Billboard,* September 29, 1953.

9. *Billboard,* October 24, 1953.

10. *Billboard,* February 20, 1954, and July 17, 1954.

11. Sean McCollum, "Those Crazy Rockin' Teenagers," *New York Times,* February 23, 1957; Richard Peterson, "Why 1955? Explaining the Advent of Rock Music," *Popular Music* 8, no. 1 (1990): 112.

12. Mike Callahan and David Edwards, "Randy Wood: The Dot Records Story," http://www.bsnpubs.com/dot/dotstory.html.

13. Peterson, "Why 1955?" 112, 113; Hall, "Whatever Happened to . . . ."

14. *Billboard,* December 11, 1943; March 19, 1955; May 21, 1955; May 28, 1955.

15. Essay on the Hilltoppers, June 30, 1955, folder 68, Mason Collection; ; Hilltopper Fan Club, bulletin 3, 1955, Mason Collection.

16. *Billboard,* June 11, 1955.

17. Hilltopper Fan Club, bulletin 4, January 15, 1956.

18. *Billboard,* January 21, 1956–January 28, 1956; February 18, 1956–March 31, 1956.

19. *Billboard,* September 15, 1956; September 22, 1956.

20. *Billboard,* February 2, 1957; March 9, 1957.

21. *Billboard,* July 15, 1957; August 12, 1957.

22. *Billboard,* August 25, 1958.

23. Jimmy Sacca, curriculum vitae; Sacca Collection, Lexington.

6. The Hilltoppers at Home and Abroad

1. Jack Spina to Bobbie Ann Mason, January 15, 1957, Mason

Collection, UA 94, box 6, folder 71; Juanita Bartlett to Bobbie Ann Mason, April 5, 1957, Mason Collection.

2. Hilltoppers Club of Great Britain, bulletin 3, March 1957, Mason Collection.

3. "The rock era—born around 1956 with Elvis Presley, peaking around 1967 with Sgt. Pepper, dying around 1976 with the Sex Pistols—turned out to be a by-way in the development of twentieth century popular music rather than, as we thought at the time, any kind of mass-cultural revolution." Frith, *Music for Pleasure,* 1. This turned out to be a double whammy against the Hilltoppers. "Do the Bop," their effort to get into the rock 'n' roll genre, not only was not good rock 'n' roll but also it was too late, as other musical genres such as country and western and hard and even acid rock became the musical fashions of the day. Increasingly, young people began to agree with author Malcolm Budd that "music is the science of sound." See Malcolm Budd, *Music and the Emotions* (London: Routledge & Kegan Paul, 1985), ix.

4. Unknown writer to Jimmy Sacca, August 10, 1957, Sacca Collection.

5. "The Hilltoppers," *Kansas City Star,* August 21, 1957.

6. "The Hilltoppers," *Kansas City Star,* August 21, 1957.

7. *National Hilltoppers Fan Club Newsletter,* September 13, 1957, Mason Collection.

8. *National Hilltoppers Fan Club Newsletter,* September 13, 1957.

9. *National Hilltoppers Fan Club Newsletter,* September 13, 1957, Mason Collection.

10. *Hilltopper Topics,* December 24, 1957, Mason Collection.

11. *Hilltopper Topics,* December 24, 1957; Summer 1958; May–June 1957, Mason Collection.

12. *Hilltopper Topics,* December 24, 1957, and Summer 1958; Don McGuire, interview by the author, April 28, 2004, Lexington.

13. *Hilltopper Topics,* Summer 1958.

14. *Hilltopper Topics,* Summer 1958.

15. *Hilltopper Topics,* Summer 1958. Of course, this impression changed over time. Many U.S. sitcoms of today got their inspiration from the BBC.

16. *Liverpool Evening Express,* May 8, 1958; *Hilltopper Topics,* Summer 1958.

17. Sue Lynn Stone, "P.S.: I Love You: The Hilltoppers," *Western Alumni Magazine,* Spring 2002; Booth, "Who Do Youth Think They Are?" 22.

18. *Hilltopper Topics,* January 1, 1959, Mason Collection.

19. Billy Reed, "Tunes for the Trip down Nostalgia Lane," *Louisville Courier-Journal,* May 19, 1975.

20. *Hilltopper Topics,* Summer 1958.

21. Don McGuire, interview.

22. *Hilltopper Topics,* January 1, 1959.

23. Ray Gaines, "Park Row Paragraphs," *Bowling Green (Ky.) Daily News,* December 15, 1958.

24. *Hilltopper Topics,* May–June, 1957.

25. Gaines, "Park Row Paragraphs."

26. Jimmy Sacca, telephone interview by the author, April 2, 2005.

27. Don McGuire, interview.

28. Jimmy Sacca, interview, April 2, 2005; Don McGuire, telephone interview by the author, April 1, 2005; Don McGuire, interview by the author, May 2, 2005, Lexington, Ky.

29. Don McGuire, letter to Bobbie Ann Mason, April 24, 1959, Mason Collection.

30. Carol Braddy, letter to the author; June 20, 2004.

31. Mason, "Reaching the Stars," 38; see also Mason, *Clear Springs,* 112. Already, fan club presidents throughout the country were being advised to send their news to David Lee Enos of Hyannis, Massachusetts (*Hilltopper Topics,* January 1959); Mason, "Reaching the Stars," 38.

32. Mason, "Reaching the Stars," 38.

33. Mason, "Reaching the Stars," 38. See also Mason, *Clear Springs,* 112. "St. James Infirmary" is a sad song about a man going to see the corpse of his lover. Popular recordings of the song included versions by Cab Calloway, Louis Armstrong, Benny Goodman, the Hall Johnson Negro Choir, the Ventures, Red Garland, and Janis Joplin. There are at least twenty versions of the song. Some historians say the theme can be traced back to St. James Hospital in London. Robwalker.net/html_docs/letterthirteen.html-55k-April 8, 2005.

34. Don McGuire, interview, April 28, 2004.

35. Don McGuire, interview, April 28, 2004.

36. *National Hilltopper Fan Club Newsletter,* January 8, 1957;

C. Janusek and N. Janusek, "Interview with Sacca and Ayres."

37. Douglas Cardoza, telephone interview by the author, April 6, 2005.

38. Penelope Spiegelman Register, email to the author, July 1, 2004.

7. Latter-Day Hilltoppers

1. Darrell Silford, "Glasgow Is Home to Billy Vaughn," *Louisville Courier-Journal,* June 27, 1965; S. Rayburn Atkins, letter to the author, January 29, 2004.

2. *Glasgow (Ky.) Daily Times,* May 22, 1965.

3. Silford, "Glasgow Is Home to Vaughn"; Cheryl Holland, "Mr. Music," *Rural Kentuckian,* January 1986, 18; Ron Mitchell, "Billy Vaughn: Musician Enjoys Semi-Retirement and Playing Dixieland," *Park City (Bowling Green, Ky.) Daily News,* July 1, 1979.

4. Silford, "Glasgow Is Home to Vaughn."

5. Holland, "Mr. Music," 18; Lowe, "Vaughn Began Quartet at Boots and Saddle."

6. David "Doc" Livingston, interview by the author, January 11, 2004; "Glasgow's Billy Vaughn Leaves Saturday for Japan Tour," *Glasgow (Ky.) Daily Times,* May 15, 1969; Lowe, "Vaughn Began Quartet at Boots and Saddle"; Livingston, interview. As noted in chapter 1, even on the Ed Sullivan show in 1952, Billy Vaughn had a receding hairline, causing him to wear his beanie as much over his forehead as he could. Over time, he began to wear a toupee. Livingston remembers one time getting off a bus in a high wind in Tokyo. The pieces of Billy's toupee "were just flying away." Though they tried to help Billy retrieve the parts, his band members were practically broken up with laughter at his predicament. Lowe, "Vaughn Began Quartet at Boots and Saddle."

7. Livingston, interview; Budd, *Music and the Emotions,,* ix.

8. *Lockport (N.Y.) Union Sun Journal,* April 22, 1969.

9. Reed, "Tunes for the Trip down Nostalgia Lane." Sacca liked to repeat a statement he had made several years before that "if the good Ol' Lord lets me come back in a second life . . . I'd like to come back and live the same life I've lived because it's just been magnificent" (*Disc Jockey's and Songwriter's Digest,* August–September, 1953, 7); C. Janusek and N. Janusek, "Interview with Sacca and Ayres," 8.

10. C. Janusek and N. Janusek, "Interview with Sacca and Ayres."

11. Jimmy Sacca, interview by the author, June 18, 2004.

12. C. Janusek and N. Janusek, "Interview with Sacca and Ayres."

13. Jimmy Sacca III, e-mail to the author, May 5, 2005.

14. The author thanks Bryan Freeman of the Western football program for this information.

15. Mikki Olmstead, "Hilltopping the Charts," *College Heights Herald,* October 22, 1998.

16. Larry Wilkerson, "Hilltoppers Play a Return Engagement on 'the Hill,'" *Louisville Courier-Journal,* November 5, 1972.

17. Wilkerson, "Hilltoppers Play Return Engagement." Suellyn, Seymour's daughter, recalls, "My dad was thrilled to sing with the group again. He was excited to ride in the parade. . . . I remember thinking that weekend that his face would surely be a smile forever." Suellyn and her family "had such a ball" that homecoming weekend, that, like her mom and dad before her, she decided to become a student at Western. Suellyn Perry, e-mail to the author, April 18, 2005.

18. C. Janusek and N. Janusek, "Interview with Sacca and Ayres."

19. C. Janusek and N. Janusek, "Interview with Sacca and Ayres."

20. *Columbus (Ohio) Herald,* July 12, 1974.

21. Reed, "Tunes for Trip down Nostalgia Lane."

22. Reed, "Tunes for Trip Down Nostalgia Lane."

23. On September 12, 1997, Gary Ransdell became the ninth president of Western Kentucky University; Vickie Stevens, "Ex Hilltopper Named to Top Alumni Job," *College Heights Herald,* November 12, 1978; Donna Crouch, "Top of the Pops," *College Heights Herald,* March 22, 1988.

24. *Louisville Courier-Journal,* May 27, 2000.

25. "Seymour Spiegelman, Original Hilltoppers Member, Dies at 56," *Park City (Bowling Green, Ky.) Daily News,* February 15, 1987; Don McGuire, interview; Alex Downing, memo to the author, March 2005.

26. Willard Thomas, letter to the author, January 17, 2004; Livingston, interview.

27. *Glasgow (Ky.) Daily Times,* September 12, 1979; "We Hate

to See Vaughn Leave," editorial, *Park City (Bowling Green, Ky.) Daily News,* October 13, 1987; Thomas to author.

28. Billy Vaughn to "Inie," April 17, 1972, Grissom collection; Billy Vaughn to Doc Livingston, January 1988; Vaughn to Livingston, August 29, 1988; Vaughn to Livingston, October 7, 1988. All letters in Livingston Collection. Vaughn usually ended his letters to Livingston with "Chromatically Yours."

29. Vaughn to Livingston, May 20, 1988; Vaughn to Livingston, April 18, 1989.

30. Vaughn to Livingston, October 7, 1988.

31. "P.S. We'll Miss You, Hilltopper," editorial, *Lexington Herald-Leader,* September 22, 1991; *Park City (Bowling Green, Ky.) Daily News,* September 29, 1991.

32. *Park City (Bowling Green, Ky.) Daily News,* September 27, 1991; Don McGuire, interview.

33. *Park City (Bowling Green, Ky.) Daily News,* September 27, 1991.

34. Sacca, curriculum vitae; State of Mississippi, Senate Concurring Resolution 605.

35. Don McGuire, National Public Radio interview by Bob Edwards, January 16, 1995.

36. Max Morath, *The NPR Curious Listener's Guide to Popular Standards* (New York: Perigee Books, 2002), ix; Starr and Waterman, *American Popular Music,* 5; Donald J. Funes and Kenneth Munson, *Musical Involvement: A Guide to Perceptive Listening* (New York: Harcourt, Brace, Jovanovich, 1975), 107.

37. Brown, "Kings of the Hill."

38. Don Edwards, "P.S. We'll Miss You, Hilltopper Billy Vaughn," *Lexington Herald-Leader,* September 30, 1991.

39. "Backstreet Boys Not State's First Hot Warblers," *Lexington Herald-Leader,* January 13, 2000.

40. "Backstreet Boys."

41. Adorno, *Sociology of Music,* 35.

42. Don McGuire, interview by Bob Edwards.

43. Terry Sacca, e-mail to the author, April 25, 2005. Jimmy Sacca III, Terry's brother, agrees with Terry's assessment of their father and also believes that their mother, Ann, should be brought into the equation. "She was the glue that held everything together. . . . She was always there for me and my brothers." Ann, and by exten-

sion, the other Hilltopper wives, always "provided a family life to come home to." Ann wrote that she experienced "deep sadness" each time Jimmy left home to go back to an engagement. "Sometimes this meant being gone as long as two or three months. . . . Regardless, the boys and I would continue to live our lives knowing that he would be back. This was something that he had to do, and I knew he wouldn't have been happy doing anything else." Ann Sacca, letter to the author, May 3, 2005.

44. Hargreaves, "Preference and Prejudice in Music," 14; Charles Black, interview by the author, January 24, 2005, Morgantown, Ky.

Bibliography

Collections

Charlotte "Coogie" Grissom Collection, Glasgow, Kentucky
Doc Livingston Collection, Bowling Green, Kentucky
Bobbie Ann Mason Collection, University Archives, Western Kentucky University
Don McGuire Collection, Lexington, Kentucky
Hilltopper Collections, University Archives, Western Kentucky University
Jimmy Sacca Collection, Lexington, Kentucky

Books and Magazines

Adorno, Theodor W. *Introduction to the Sociology of Music.* New York: Seabury, 1976.

Aquila, Richard. *That Old Time Rock & Roll: A Chronicle of an Era, 1954–1963.* New York: Schirmer Books, 1989.

Billboard. December 11, 1943; October 25, 1952; November 1, 1952; September 29, 1953; March 19, 1955; May 21, 1955; May 28, 1955; June 11, 1955; January 15, 1956; January 28, 1956; September 22, 1956; February 2, 1957.

Booth, Daniel. "Who Do Youth Think They Are?" *Melody Maker,* May 15, 1999, 22–23.

Brackett, David. "The Politics and Practice of 'Crossover' in American Popular Music, 1963 to 1965." *Musical Quarterly* 78, no. 4 (Winter 1994): 774–97.

Brown, Katherine. "Kings of the Hill." *Kentucky Monthly,* December 1999, 15–17.

Brown, Tony. "The Bane of Show Business." *Picturegoer,* August 11, 1956.

Budd, Malcolm. *Music and the Emotions.* London: Routledge & Kegan Paul, 1985.

Chevigny, Paul. *Gigs: Jazz and the Cabaret Laws in New York City.* New York: Routledge, 1991.

Cooper, B. Lee. *Images of American Society in Popular Music: A Guide to Reflective Teaching.* Chicago: Nelson-Hall, 1982.

Crunden, Robert M. *A Brief History of American Culture.* Armonk, N.Y.: M. E. Sharpe, 1996.

Dampier, Don J. *Finding the Fifties.* Georgetown, Ky.: DJ Discovery Press, 2005.

Disc Jockey's and Songwriter's Digest, August–September, 1953.

Epstein, Jonathan. *Adolescents and Their Music: If It's Too Loud, You're Too Old.* New York: Garland, 1994.

Frith, Simon. *Music for Pleasure: Essays in the Sociology of Pop.* New York: Routledge, 1988.

Funes, Donald J., and Kenneth Munson. *Musical Involvement: A Guide to Perceptive Listening.* New York: Harcourt, Brace & Jovanovich, 1975.

"Grouped for Stardom." *Hit Parader,* June 1957.

Hargreaves, David J. "Preference and Prejudice in Music: A Psychological Approach." *Popular Music and Society* 8, no. 2 (1982): 14.

Harrison, Lowell. *Western Kentucky University.* Lexington: University Press of Kentucky, 1987.

Hesbacker, Peter. "Record World and Billboard Charts Compared: Single Hits, 1970–1979." *Popular Music & Society* 8, no. 2 (1982): 101.

Hilltopper-ette Topics, 1953.

Hilltopper Club of Great Britain, January 15, 1956; July 27, 1956; March 1957.

Hilltopper Fanzine, 1953–58.

Hilltopper Topics, January–February, 1957; March–April, 1957; May–June, 1957; September 13, 1957; January 1, 1959.

"The Hilltoppers Are Back!" *Record Whirl,* June 1955, 12–13.

"The Hilltoppers Are Hit-Toppers," *In Kentucky,* Winter 1952–53, 37–42.

"The Hilltoppers Come to Town," *Musical Express* (London), July 13, 1956.

Holland, Cheryl. "Mr. Music: Billy Vaughn Has Never Been a Superstar but His Records Have Sold in the Millions." *Rural Kentuckian,* January 1986, 17–18.

Jackson, Carlton. *J. I. Rodale: Apostle of Nonconformity.* New York: Pyramid Press, 1974.

Jackson, John A. *American Bandstand: Dick Clark and the Making of a Rock 'n' Roll Empire.* New York: Oxford University Press, 1997.

Janusek, Carl, and Nancy Janusek. Interview with Jimmy Sacca and Chuck Ayre. *Discoveries,* May 1992.

Jeckell, Barry A., and Tamara Conniff. "It's a Music Revolution." *USA Weekend,* February 24–26, 2006.

Kammen, Michael. *American Culture, American Tastes: Social Change and the 20th Century.* New York: Basic Books, 1999.

Maddox, Greg. "A Little Touch of Magic." *Bowling Green Magazine,* Fall/Winter, 1986, 26–27.

Mason, Bobbie Ann. *Clear Springs: A Memoir.* New York: Random House, 1999.

———. "Reaching the Stars: My Life as a Fifties Groupie." *New Yorker,* May 26, 1986.

McClanahan, Ed. *Famous People I Have Known.* New York: Farrar, Strauss, Giroux, 1985.

Miller, James. *Flowers in the Dustbin: The Rise of Rock and Roll.* New York: Simon & Schuster, 1999.

Morath, Max. *The NPR Curious Listener's Guide to Popular Standards.* New York: Perigee Books, 2002.

Nite, Norm N. *Rock On: The Illustrated Encyclopedia of Rock 'n' Roll,* vol. 1. New York: Thomas Y. Crowell, 1992.

Peterson, Richard. "Why 1955? Explaining the Advent of Rock Music." *Popular Music* 9, no. 1(January 1990): 97–117.

"Rise of the Hilltoppers," *Newsweek,* November 10, 1952.

Rodnitzky, J. "A Rocky Road to Respect: Trends in Academic Writing on Popular Music." *Popular Music and Society* 21, Spring 1997: 93–96.

Rowe, David. *Popular Cultures: Rock Music, Sport, and the Politics of Pleasure.* London: Sage, 1995.

Sanjek, Russell. *Pennies from Heaven: The American Popular Music Business in the 20th Century.* New York: Da Capo Press, 1996.

Scott, Cheryl. "Begin the Beguine." *Western Alumni Magazine,* November 30, 1950; Winter 1981; Spring 2002, 4–6.

Sloboda, John A. *The Musical Mind: The Cognitive Psychology of Music*. Oxford: Clarendon Press, 1985.

The Stage, July 12, 1956.

Starr, Larry, and Christopher Waterman. *American Popular Music: From Minstrelsy to MTV.* New York: Oxford University Press, 2003.

Stebbins, Robert A. *The Barbershop Singer: Inside the Social World of Musical Hobby.* Buffalo, N.Y.: University of Toronto Press, 1996.

Stierle, Wayne. "The Fine Art of Covering Hits." *Rock Magazine,* September 10, 1973.

———. "The Hilltoppers: From Hit Pop to Vanishing Act." *Goldmine,* November 6, 1987.

Teenage Voice, June 1957, 7.

"They're Really Teenagers at Heart; the Hilltoppers." *Recordland,* September 1954, 28–29.

Tocqueville, Alexis de. *Democracy in America.* Ed. J. P. Mayer; 12th ed. New York: Anchor Books, 1969.

"Topping 'Em All, the Hilltoppers." *Hit Parader,* August 1957.

TV Mirror, July 21, 1956. September 1, 1956; September 15, 1956.

Warner, Jay. "The Hilltoppers." In *The Billboard Book of American Singing Groups: A History, 1940–1990.* New York: Billboard Books, 1992.

Weekly News (England), Apri1 11, 1956.

What's On (England); July 13, 1956.

Zabe, "Formed by Accident, Hilltoppers Still Operate on Part-Time Basis," *Downbeat,* February 10, 1954, 3.

Index